L.S. SMITH

Quiet the Spiral

Break Free from Overthinking, Calm Anxiety, and Reclaim Your Peace of Mind

For every overthinker who has ever stared at the ceiling at 2 a.m., replaying conversations you can't change or worrying about futures that haven't happened yet—this book is for you.

For those who have felt the weight of "too much" in their own minds, who've lost sleep, missed joy, or doubted their worth—you are not broken. You are human. May these pages remind you that peace is possible, and your spiral does not define your story. You deserve a life of calm, courage, and freedom.

"Peace is not the absence of thought, but the power to choose which thoughts you follow."

L.S. SMITH

Contents

Acknowledgments

Writing this book was not a solitary act. It was shaped by the countless stories, conversations, and small moments of honesty I've been entrusted with over the years. To every client, reader, and friend who has said, *"I thought it was just me"*—thank you. Your vulnerability lit the way for this work.

To my husband, who has listened patiently through both my spirals and my chapters, thank you for being the steady ground beneath my feet. Your calm has been the mirror that reminded me what peace looks like.

To my family, whose love has been my anchor even in stormy seasons, thank you for reminding me that life is not about perfection, but presence.

To my friends, who sent encouraging texts, shared belly laughs, and reminded me that joy is the best antidote to overthinking—this book carries your fingerprints on every page.

And finally, to every reader holding this book now: thank you. Thank you for your courage in facing your own spirals, for daring to believe that peace is possible, and for inviting my words into your life. This book isn't complete without you—you are the reason it exists.

Introduction

Welcome to the Spiral

It usually starts quietly.

You replay something you said earlier that day. *Did I sound rude? Did they take it the wrong way? Should I have explained myself differently?* At first, the thought feels small, like a loose thread on a sweater. But the more you tug at it, the more it unravels. Before you know it, you're stuck in an endless loop of "what ifs," "should haves," and "maybes."

The spiral tightens. Sleep slips away. Your chest feels heavy. By morning, nothing is solved—yet you're exhausted, as if you ran an all-night marathon you never signed up for.

Sound familiar? If it does, you're far from alone.

Why We Spiral

Overthinking has become one of the most common struggles of our time. Surveys show that **73% of adults between the ages of 25 and 35** identify themselves as "chronic overthinkers," and nearly half of adults over 35 say the same. It cuts across generations, careers, and cultures.

Why? Because modern life bombards us with stimuli our brains weren't designed to handle.

- We're inundated with information—emails, texts, news alerts, social media feeds—all demanding mental space.
- We face an endless series of decisions, from the trivial (*What should I eat?*) to the life-altering (*Should I change jobs?*).
- We live under pressure to succeed, compare, and constantly perform—at work, in relationships, even in how we present ourselves online.

Our brains evolved to scan for danger and solve problems. But when the "danger" is an awkward pause in a meeting or a delayed reply to a text, the survival system still kicks in. The result is the spiral: your mind believes that replaying, analyzing, and predicting will protect you. Instead, it traps you.

You Are Not Broken

Here's something I want you to hold onto from the very beginning: **you are not broken.**

Overthinking isn't a flaw in your character. It isn't weakness. It's your brain trying too hard to protect you. That instinct once kept our ancestors alive— but today, it leaves us stuck.

The spiral is not who you are. It's something you experience. And if you can experience it, you can change your relationship with it.

The Cost of Living in the Spiral

Before we talk about solutions, let's be honest about the price you've already paid.

- **Lost time.** Hours, even days, swallowed by rumination.
- **Sleepless nights.** Spirals love the quiet hours, when there's nothing left

to distract you.

- **Strained relationships.** Overthinking makes you second-guess, withdraw, or misinterpret others.
- **Exhaustion.** Even when you haven't "done" anything, your brain feels like it ran a marathon.
- **Missed opportunities.** The spiral convinces you to hesitate, stall, or avoid taking risks.

Maybe you recognize yourself in one of these. Maybe in all of them.

Here's the hard truth: overthinking steals life from the present moment. But here's the hopeful truth: you can take it back.

What This Book Is—and Isn't

This book isn't about "stopping thoughts" or "emptying your mind." That's not only unrealistic—it's impossible. You don't want to shut off your thoughts. They're how you dream, imagine, and create.

Instead, this book is about:

- Learning to notice the spiral without being consumed by it.
- Recognizing that not every thought deserves your attention.
- Using simple, practical tools to step out of overthinking and into clarity.
- Building habits that create space for peace—even in stressful times.

Each chapter offers a piece of the puzzle: awareness, reframing, calming the body, taking action, decluttering, setting thought boundaries, practicing self-compassion, building resilience, and carrying peace into everyday life.

By the time you finish, you'll have a toolkit you can reach for anytime the spiral starts.

A Story of the Spiral

Let me tell you about *Michael*.

Michael was a manager at a tech company, known for his attention to detail. But his greatest strength was also his greatest struggle. He replayed every meeting in his head, worried constantly about how his team perceived him, and lost sleep over every email he sent.

One night, he stayed awake until 2 a.m., convinced he'd made a mistake in a quarterly report. He imagined his boss discovering it, imagined being reprimanded, imagined losing his job. His chest tightened, his thoughts raced, and by morning, he was drained. When he opened the report to check—there was no mistake.

Michael's story isn't unique. It's the spiral at work: a loop of worry that feels urgent but solves nothing.

Now imagine Michael with tools. Instead of replaying the report in his head, he notices the spiral beginning and names it: *"This is worry."* He pauses, takes three slow breaths, and grounds himself in the present. He reframes the thought: *"I worked carefully on this. If there's an error, I can fix it. One report won't define my career."* His body calms, his mind clears, and he falls asleep.

That shift—from drowning in the spiral to stepping out of it—is what this book is about.

Exercise: Your Spiral Snapshot

Before we go further, take a moment to personalize this.

Grab a notebook (or the journal in the back of this book) and write down:

- The last time you caught yourself spiraling.
- What triggered it.
- How it felt in your body.
- How long it lasted.

Then, at the bottom, write this sentence:

"I am not my spiral."

This simple declaration will become your anchor throughout this journey.

A Gentle Promise

I want to make you a promise: this book is not about perfection. You won't erase overthinking forever. Spirals will still appear. But they will no longer own you.

You'll notice them sooner. They'll feel less overwhelming. And you'll have tools to step out and return to calm.

Progress may be gradual. Some days will feel easier than others. But every small shift—every breath you take, every spiral you interrupt, every moment of peace you create—is a victory.

Moving Forward

Here's what you can expect as we continue:

- In **Part One**, we'll understand the spiral—what overthinking is, why anxiety fuels it, and what it costs you.
- In **Part Two**, we'll learn how to break the spiral with awareness, reframing, calming the body, and small actions.
- In **Part Three**, we'll build habits that sustain a calmer mind—decluttering,

setting boundaries with thoughts, and reclaiming your inner voice.

- In **Part Four**, we'll explore resilience, mindfulness in daily life, and how to live boldly with calm at your core.

By the end, you'll not only know how to quiet the spiral—you'll know how to live with clarity, strength, and peace.

So, take a breath. You've already started.

By picking up this book, you've said: *I don't want to live inside the spiral anymore. I want something different.*

That intention matters. It's the first step toward reclaiming your mind and your life.

Let's begin. Together, we'll quiet the spiral.

The Anatomy of Overthinking

It begins with a single thought.

Maybe it's something small, like *Did I lock the door?* or *Did I sound weird in that text?* At first, it feels harmless. But then the thought loops: *What if I didn't lock it? What if someone breaks in? What if they think I'm rude? What if they don't like me anymore?*

In just a few minutes, your brain has spun from a simple question to a full-blown disaster scenario. That's overthinking in action.

What Is Overthinking?

At its core, overthinking is the habit of replaying, analyzing, and predicting in endless loops without reaching resolution. It's the mind's attempt to prepare, but instead of solving problems, it multiplies them.

Think of it like being stuck on a treadmill. Your legs move, your energy drains, but you never actually get anywhere. Overthinking gives the *illusion* of progress while keeping you stuck in place.

Researchers define overthinking as a combination of **rumination** (rehashing the past) and **worry** (projecting into the future). Rumination sounds like: *"Why did I say that? I should've done it differently."* Worry sounds like: *"What if I fail? What if something goes wrong?"*

Together, they create the spiral.

Why We Do It

Overthinking is not laziness or weakness. It's actually your brain trying to keep you safe.

Humans evolved with a survival mechanism called the **threat-detection system.**

Thousands of years ago, it kept our ancestors alive. If you heard a rustle in the bushes, your brain raced through possibilities: *Predator? Enemy? Storm?* That vigilance increased your chances of survival.

The problem is, our modern environment doesn't match our ancient wiring. Today, the rustle in the bushes is an unread email, a delayed text, or a meeting with your boss. There's no lion—but your brain still reacts as if your life is on the line.

Your mind spins because it believes that analyzing every angle will protect you. But instead of preventing danger, it traps you in imagined ones.

The Spiral Metaphor

Picture a spiral staircase.

At the top step, you start with a simple thought: *I made a mistake.*
  One step down: *What if I get in trouble?*
  Another step: *What if I lose my job?*
  Another: *What if I can't pay my bills?*
  At the bottom: *What if I end up with nothing?*

You've descended ten floors in less than ten seconds. That's the speed of the spiral.

And because it feels urgent, you keep circling, as if the bottom step holds an answer. But there is no answer—just endless loops.

The Signs You're Overthinking

You may be caught in the spiral if you:

- Rehearse conversations in your head long after they're over.
- Struggle to fall asleep because your mind won't shut off.
- Second-guess even small decisions.
- Obsessively predict how situations might play out.
- Feel paralyzed, unable to act because you're still "analyzing."

Sound familiar? You're not alone. Studies show that overthinking is one of the most common mental traps—affecting nearly everyone at some point.

How Overthinking Affects the Body

Overthinking isn't just mental—it shows up in your body too. Spirals can trigger:

- Racing heartbeat
- Muscle tension
- Stomach upset
- Headaches
- Restless energy
- Insomnia

That's because overthinking activates the **stress response**. The body reacts as if there's real danger, pumping out stress hormones like cortisol. The longer the spiral continues, the more drained you feel—mentally and physically.

Story: Anna's Night Spiral

Anna was a graduate student who often stayed up late replaying conversations. One night, she found herself stuck thinking about a class presentation. She replayed every word, imagining her professor's disapproval, her classmates' judgment, even her future career crumbling.

By 3 a.m., her body was buzzing with adrenaline, though she was lying in bed. She was exhausted but couldn't turn it off. When she finally presented the next day, it went fine. Her professor even complimented her.

Anna realized afterward: the spiral hadn't prepared her—it had punished her. She spent an entire night suffering over something that never happened.

Why It's Hard to Stop

Here's the paradox: telling yourself *"stop overthinking"* never works. In fact, it makes things worse.

Psychologists call this the **white bear effect.** If I say: *"Don't think of a white bear,"* what happens? A white bear pops instantly into your mind. The more you try not to think about something, the stronger it becomes.

That's why brute force doesn't work. Overthinking isn't solved by resisting thoughts—it's solved by changing your relationship to them.

Guided Practice: Draw Your Spiral

Take a blank piece of paper. Without overthinking it (yes, I know), draw what your spiral feels like.

- Maybe it's a whirlpool dragging you down.
- Maybe it's a staircase circling tighter.

- Maybe it's just a scribble that keeps looping.

There's no wrong way to do this. The point isn't art—it's awareness.

When you finish, write at the bottom:

"I can step out of this spiral."

This practice gives shape to something invisible. Once you see your spiral on paper, it feels less like *you* and more like a *pattern*—a pattern you can change.

Reflection Questions

- What does your spiral usually sound like—rumination (past) or worry (future)?
- When does it show up most often (bedtime, mornings, social interactions, work)?
- What does your body feel like when you're spiraling?

Jotting down your answers builds awareness. Remember: you can't change what you don't notice.

Key Takeaway

Overthinking is not who you are—it's a survival instinct misfiring in the modern world. It drains your energy, creates false stories, and pulls you away from the present moment. But once you understand its anatomy, you can begin to loosen its grip.

The next chapter will explore how anxiety fuels the spiral—and why noticing its physical signs is a critical step in breaking free.

Anxiety's Grip

If overthinking is the spiral, anxiety is the motor that keeps it spinning.

Think back to the last time you couldn't stop replaying something in your mind. Maybe it was a conversation where you worried you sounded foolish. Or maybe it was the uncertainty of waiting—waiting for a test result, waiting for a text, waiting for feedback on a project.

The thoughts weren't just mental. They came with a rush of physical sensations: a racing heart, a tight chest, a restless energy you couldn't shake. That's anxiety at work. It doesn't just live in your mind—it takes over your body too. And once it does, it feeds the spiral of overthinking until you feel stuck in both.

What Anxiety Really Is

Anxiety is often misunderstood. Many people think of it as weakness, or as something that should be suppressed or ignored. But at its core, anxiety is simply your body's alarm system.

It exists to protect you. When your brain perceives a threat, it activates the **fight-or-flight response**: your heart rate rises, adrenaline floods your system, your muscles tense, your breathing quickens. This makes sense if you're about to face a tiger in the wild. Your body is preparing you to run or defend yourself.

The problem is, in our modern lives, the "tigers" are rarely life-threatening. They're usually emails, deadlines, awkward pauses, or uncertain futures. But your nervous system can't tell the difference. It reacts the same way—flipping on the alarm for things that don't actually require it.

And once the alarm is ringing, your mind races to justify it. *Why is my chest tight? Why is my heart pounding? Something must be wrong. I need to figure this out.* That loop is the start of the spiral.

The Anxiety–Overthinking Cycle

Here's how the cycle usually works:

1. **Trigger:** Something sparks uncertainty—a late email, a frown from your boss, a strange ache in your body.
2. **Anxiety response:** The body reacts. Heart races, breath shortens, adrenaline surges.
3. **Thought spiral:** The mind jumps in to explain the feelings. *What if it's bad? What if I did something wrong?*
4. **Fuel:** The thoughts increase anxiety, which fuels more thoughts. Round and round it goes.

It's like being on a hamster wheel powered by fear—you run faster and faster but never get anywhere.

How Anxiety Shows Up

Anxiety can look different for everyone, but here are some common ways it grips both body and mind:

- **In the body:** racing heart, shallow breath, sweaty palms, tight stomach, tense muscles, shaky hands.
- **In the mind:** constant worry, jumping to worst-case scenarios, obsessing

over details, difficulty concentrating, replaying conversations.

- **In behavior:** avoiding situations, procrastinating, needing constant reassurance, withdrawing from others.

Often, people don't even realize their physical symptoms are anxiety. They think they're "just stressed" or "just tired." But when you connect the dots, you start to see how much anxiety shapes your daily life.

Why Anxiety Feels So Powerful

Anxiety feels overwhelming because it's primal. It's wired deep into the nervous system. You can't logic your way out of it when your body is convinced you're in danger. That's why overthinking and anxiety are such close partners. The anxious body sends signals to the brain, and the brain scrambles to make sense of them, often through endless analysis.

It's not "all in your head." It's in your body too.

Story: Rachel and the Elevator

Rachel hated elevators. Every time she stepped inside, her chest tightened, her palms grew damp, and her thoughts raced. *What if it gets stuck? What if I can't breathe? What if I panic in front of everyone?*

Her anxiety triggered physical symptoms, which triggered spiraling thoughts, which intensified the anxiety—a feedback loop that left her avoiding elevators altogether.

When she finally learned that what she was experiencing was her body's alarm system—not a sign of real danger—something shifted. She began practicing deep breathing before stepping inside, labeling the experience: *"This is anxiety, not reality."* Over time, the grip loosened.

Her story is a reminder: the spiral feels convincing, but it isn't always true.

Identifying Triggers

One of the most empowering steps in loosening anxiety's grip is learning your personal triggers. These are the sparks that light the spiral.

Common triggers include:

- Social situations (fear of judgment or embarrassment)
- Work deadlines or performance pressure
- Money and financial worries
- Health concerns or unfamiliar symptoms
- Relationships (fear of rejection or conflict)
- Uncertainty or lack of control

Your triggers may be different. The important thing is to notice them—not so you can avoid them, but so you can meet them with awareness.

Exercise: Map Your Anxiety Spiral

Turn to your journal in the back of this book and try this exercise:

1. Draw a circle in the center of the page and label it **"Anxiety."**
2. Around it, draw smaller circles for your common triggers—things that often set off spirals.
3. From each trigger, draw arrows to the thoughts and body sensations it creates.

- Example: Trigger = "Work email from boss." Thoughts = *"I must have done something wrong."* Body = racing heart.

When you finish, look at the map. See the connections. This exercise helps you realize anxiety doesn't come out of nowhere—it follows patterns. And patterns can be interrupted.

At the bottom of the page, write this reminder:

"Anxiety is the fuel, not the truth."

A Body in Alarm Mode

When anxiety grips you, it's as if your body has pressed the "panic button." Imagine your nervous system as a smoke alarm. It's meant to warn you of fire—but sometimes it goes off when you burn toast.

The alarm is loud, frightening, and feels urgent. But the sound itself isn't proof of danger. Anxiety is the same way. Just because your body feels unsafe doesn't mean you actually are.

This distinction is crucial: **you can feel anxious without being in danger.**

Building Awareness of the Grip

The first step in loosening anxiety's grip is simply noticing it. Pay attention to the moments when anxiety shows up in your body. Does your chest tighten before a meeting? Does your jaw clench when you get a text? Do your thoughts race when you lie down at night?

Noticing the grip is the beginning of breaking it. Because once you can name it—*"This is anxiety"*—you create space to respond instead of being swept away.

Reflection: My Anxiety Pattern

Take a moment to reflect on these questions:

- When does anxiety show up most often for me?
- What are my most common physical symptoms?
- How do my thoughts respond to those sensations?

Write down your answers. Awareness is power—it turns invisible patterns into visible ones.

Key Takeaway

Anxiety is not your enemy—it's your body's alarm system. But when it misfires, it fuels the spiral of overthinking. By identifying your triggers and learning to label anxiety as fuel—not fact—you begin to loosen its grip.

In the next chapter, we'll explore the hidden costs of living in the spiral—and why reclaiming your peace is one of the greatest gifts you can give yourself.

The Hidden Cost of Mental Noise

At first, overthinking feels harmless. You're "just being careful." You tell yourself you're preparing, being responsible, making sure you don't miss anything. It feels like a strength—the sign of someone who cares, someone who tries hard.

But here's the truth: overthinking is never free.

Every spiral comes with a cost, and often a bigger one than we realize. It steals time, drains energy, strains relationships, erodes confidence, and quietly robs us of joy. By the time we recognize what's happening, the spiral has already taken hours—or years—of our lives.

This chapter is about looking those costs in the eye. Not to feel guilt or shame, but to wake up. Because once you see what the spiral is stealing, you can make a conscious choice to take it back.

The Illusion of Productivity

One of the biggest lies of overthinking is that it feels like doing something.

When you replay a conversation for the tenth time, it feels like you're preparing for the next one. When you analyze every angle of a decision, it feels like you're being thorough. When you predict all the possible outcomes of a situation, it feels like you're being responsible.

But here's the reality: you're not solving the problem—you're circling it.

Overthinking is like running on a treadmill. You sweat, you strain, you move—but you never actually get anywhere. Worse, when you step off, you're exhausted with nothing to show for it.

The True Costs of Overthinking

Let's break down the hidden price you pay when you live in the spiral.

1. Time

Overthinking devours time you can never get back. A decision that could take five minutes stretches into an entire evening. A single "what if" can eat up hours of replaying and predicting. Weeks slip by while you hesitate to act.

And the cruel irony? Even after all that time, you often feel less certain than when you began.

2. Sleep

Spirals love bedtime. The moment the world goes quiet, your mind gets loud. Thoughts you managed to push aside all day come roaring back. *What if I said the wrong thing? What if tomorrow goes badly?*

The result? Restless nights, groggy mornings, and days lived in a fog. Sleep deprivation then fuels more anxiety, which fuels more spirals—a vicious cycle that leaves you exhausted.

3. Energy

Thinking burns energy. Your brain is only 2% of your body weight, but it consumes about 20% of your daily energy. When you spiral, your brain is burning fuel nonstop, often without producing anything useful. No wonder you feel drained even when you haven't "done" much.

4. Relationships

Overthinking doesn't just affect you—it affects the people around you. Maybe you withdraw from loved ones because you're trapped in your head. Maybe you overanalyze every word your partner says, creating tension where none existed. Maybe you miss moments with your kids because you're distracted by loops of worry.

   Over time, this erodes connection. The spiral builds walls where there should be bridges.

5. Confidence

The more you second-guess yourself, the less you trust your own judgment. And when you don't trust yourself, you hesitate. You seek reassurance. You avoid risks. Slowly, your confidence wears away, leaving you dependent on external validation instead of your own inner compass.

6. Joy

Perhaps the greatest cost of all: overthinking steals the present moment.

While your body is here, your mind is stuck in yesterday or tomorrow. You miss the joy of laughing with friends, savoring a meal, or noticing a sunset because your attention is hijacked by the spiral.

And joy doesn't come back later. Missed moments are gone.

Story: David's Vacation

David had looked forward to his family vacation for months. But when he got there, he found himself consumed by spirals.

Did I forget to send that work email? What if the office needs me? What if the trip is costing too much? What if something goes wrong while we're away?

He sat on the beach, surrounded by beauty and laughter—and felt none of it. His body was on vacation, but his mind was still in the office, still worrying about money, still stuck in "what ifs."

When he came home, he realized he hadn't actually enjoyed the trip. He had missed the moments in front of him. The spiral had stolen them.

The Emotional Toll

Beyond time, energy, and sleep, overthinking takes an emotional toll:

- **Guilt** for not being present with loved ones.
- **Frustration** at yourself for "not being able to stop."
- **Hopelessness** from feeling stuck in a loop you can't escape.
- **Shame** when you compare yourself to others who seem calmer.

This emotional weight often deepens the spiral. You start overthinking about your overthinking: *Why can't I get this under control? What's wrong with me?*

But remember: nothing is wrong with you. Overthinking is a learned pattern, and patterns can be unlearned.

Exercise: The Spiral's Price Tag

Turn to your journal and divide a page into four boxes. Label them:

- **Time**
- **Energy**
- **Relationships**
- **Joy**

Under each heading, write one way overthinking has cost you in that area.

For example:

- *Time:* "Spent an entire Saturday worrying instead of relaxing."
- *Energy:* "Felt drained after replaying a conversation all night."
- *Relationships:* "Ignored my partner at dinner because I was stuck in my head."
- *Joy:* "Missed enjoying my kid's soccer game because I was worrying about work."

When you finish, look at the page. Seeing the costs in black and white is eye-opening.

At the bottom, write this statement:

"I am worth more than what my spiral steals."

Why Facing the Cost Matters

You may be tempted to skip this exercise. After all, it's not fun to confront what you've lost. But awareness of the cost is essential. If the spiral feels like "no big deal," you won't have motivation to change.

When you recognize that overthinking is stealing your most precious resources—time, energy, confidence, connection, joy—you begin to see why it's worth fighting for your peace.

Reflection: The Opportunity Cost

Think of one moment in your life where overthinking stole your presence. What could you have experienced if you hadn't been spiraling? Connection? Rest? Fun?

Now imagine reclaiming even a fraction of that energy moving forward. What could you create? How much lighter would you feel?

Overthinking isn't just costing you in the past—it's costing you in the present and the future.

A Wake-Up Call and an Invitation

It's time to be honest with yourself. Overthinking has already taken enough. But it doesn't have to keep taking.

By facing the cost now, you give yourself permission to take your life back. You can reclaim your time, your energy, your confidence, your joy.

And that's exactly what we'll do in the chapters ahead.

Key Takeaway

Overthinking doesn't protect you—it robs you. It takes time, sleep, energy, relationships, confidence, and joy. Seeing the spiral's true cost is the first step toward change.

In the next chapter, we'll begin breaking the spiral by learning how to pause the spin with one powerful tool: awareness.

Pause the Spin: The Power of Awareness

The first step out of the spiral is not control. It's not fixing. It's not even "thinking positive."

It's awareness.

Awareness is like turning on the light in a dark room. The furniture doesn't vanish, but suddenly you see it clearly—and with clarity, you stop bumping into things. In the same way, awareness doesn't erase thoughts, but it changes how you relate to them. And that shift changes everything.

Why Awareness Matters

When you're lost in overthinking, you're fused with your thoughts. They feel like reality. *I messed up. Everyone thinks I'm incompetent. This will ruin everything.*

In those moments, there's no separation between you and your spiral. You don't have a thought—you *are* the thought.

Awareness breaks that fusion. It gives you just enough space to say: *"I'm noticing that I'm spiraling right now."* That single pause loosens the grip. It interrupts the automatic loop and reminds you: you are more than your thoughts.

Psychologists call this **meta-cognition**—the ability to think about your thinking. Mindfulness traditions call it "the observer's seat." Whatever name you give it, the effect is the same: awareness is the first tool for quieting the spiral.

The Science of Naming

Research shows that when we **label emotions or thought patterns**, their intensity decreases. Neuroscientist Matthew Lieberman famously described this as "name it to tame it."

Here's why: emotions and spirals activate the brain's amygdala, the fear center. But when you put feelings into words, you engage the prefrontal cortex—the part of the brain responsible for reasoning and perspective. Simply saying, *"This is worry,"* helps shift activity away from panic and toward clarity.

It's not magic—it's neuroscience.

"Name It to Tame It" in Practice

When you notice your thoughts racing, try this:

1. Pause.
2. Say to yourself (out loud if possible): *"This is worry."* or *"This is replaying."* or *"This is predicting."*
3. Take a slow breath.
4. Remind yourself: *"It's just a thought. Not the truth. Not a command."*

The goal isn't to stop the thought. It's to see it for what it is: a mental event, not reality.

Story: Sarah's Meeting Spiral

Sarah dreaded weekly staff meetings. After each one, she replayed her comments endlessly. *Did I sound stupid? Did I interrupt someone? Did they think I was unprepared?*

The spiral stole her entire afternoon. One day, she tried something new. As her thoughts started racing, she whispered: *"This is me worrying."*

That tiny act gave her space. She took a breath, looked around the room, and realized: no one else seemed upset. The meeting had moved on. Awareness didn't erase her worries, but it loosened them. By naming the spiral, she had stepped outside of it.

The Observer Metaphor

Imagine you're sitting in a theater, watching a movie of your thoughts. The scenes flash by—conversations, worries, predictions. Normally, you forget you're in the audience. You get sucked into the story, as if it's real life.

Awareness is remembering: *I'm the one in the seat, not the movie on the screen.*

When you take the observer's seat, you see thoughts as passing images—not as commands you have to obey.

A Three-Minute Awareness Practice

Here's a simple exercise you can do anytime, anywhere:

1. **Pause.** Stop whatever you're doing and close your eyes.
2. **Breathe.** Inhale through your nose for four counts. Exhale for six. Do this twice.
3. **Name It.** Silently say: *"This is overthinking."* or *"This is anxiety."*

4. **Anchor.** Bring your focus to your senses. Name three things you see, two things you hear, one thing you feel.

That's it. Three minutes. The spiral loses momentum the moment you notice it.

Common Myths About Awareness

- **"If I notice my thoughts, they'll get louder."**
- Actually, the opposite is true. Noticing deflates their urgency.
- **"Awareness means judging myself."**
- No. Awareness is neutral—like a scientist observing data.
- **"I need to clear my mind completely."**
- Impossible. The goal isn't an empty mind. It's a spacious one.

Story: James and the Insomnia Spiral

James often lay awake at night, spiraling about work. The more he told himself, *"Don't think about it, just sleep,"* the more his thoughts raced.

Then he tried awareness. Instead of resisting, he named it: *"I'm noticing worry."* He pictured himself stepping back, watching the thoughts float by. The pressure eased. His body relaxed. Sleep finally came.

James learned that awareness wasn't about shutting down thoughts—it was about loosening their grip.

Exercise: Spiral Spotting

For the next 24 hours, play detective with your mind. Each time you notice a spiral starting, jot it down in your journal:

- What triggered it?

- What did the spiral sound like?
- How did your body feel?

At the end of the day, review your notes. You'll start to see patterns—triggers, themes, times of day. Awareness grows with practice, and with growth comes freedom.

Reflection: The Light Switch

Think back to a recent spiral. Imagine if, in that moment, you had paused and said: *"This is worry."* How might the experience have changed?

Awareness is the light switch. The spiral may not vanish, but it no longer leaves you stumbling in the dark.

Key Takeaway

You don't have to fight your thoughts—you only have to notice them. Awareness interrupts the spiral by creating space between you and your mind. Naming the spiral is the first step toward taming it.

In the next chapter, we'll build on awareness with another tool: shifting the lens—reframing anxious thoughts into clearer, more balanced perspectives.

Shift the Lens: From Worry to Perspective

Imagine looking through a camera lens. If the lens is cracked, smudged, or zoomed too far in, the picture comes out distorted. But when you adjust the lens, the image sharpens into clarity.

Overthinking works the same way. When you're caught in a spiral, your mental "lens" tilts toward fear and exaggeration. A neutral event feels like catastrophe. A small mistake feels like the end of everything. The situation itself isn't always as bad as it feels—it's the way you're looking at it.

The good news? Lenses can shift.

Why Reframing Matters

Your brain is a meaning-making machine. Every day, it takes neutral events and spins them into stories. The problem is, under the influence of anxiety and overthinking, those stories skew negative.

- A coworker walks by without saying hello.
- Story one: *She must be upset with me.*
- Story two: *She's probably distracted and didn't notice.*
- You stumble over a sentence in a meeting.
- Story one: *Everyone thinks I'm incompetent.*
- Story two: *I kept going, and no one noticed nearly as much as I did.*

Same event. Two possible lenses. One drives the spiral, the other brings peace.

Reframing doesn't mean pretending everything is fine. It means shifting from distortion to balance.

The Brain's Negativity Bias

Neuroscience offers an explanation for why our lenses so often tilt negative: the **negativity bias.**

Human brains are wired to notice threats more than neutral or positive things. From an evolutionary standpoint, this made sense—missing a danger could cost your life, while missing a pleasant flower had no consequence.

Today, this bias means we tend to:

- Dwell on criticism more than praise.
- Remember failures more vividly than successes.
- Assume worst-case scenarios when information is unclear.

Overthinking is the negativity bias on overdrive. Reframing is how we balance it.

Fact, Fear, or Fiction?

One powerful reframing tool is the **Fact–Fear–Fiction filter.**

When you catch yourself spiraling, ask:

- **Fact:** What is verifiably true?
- **Fear:** What part of this thought is anxiety speaking?
- **Fiction:** What part have I created or exaggerated?

Example: *"My friend hasn't texted me back. She must be angry with me."*

- Fact: *She hasn't texted back.*
- Fear: *She's upset with me.*
- Fiction: *She's ending our friendship.*

When you separate facts from fears and fictions, you stop treating every anxious thought as truth.

Story: Kevin's Performance Review

Kevin dreaded performance reviews. Before one meeting, his spiral began: *What if my boss is disappointed? What if I'm on thin ice? What if I lose my job?*

When he practiced Fact–Fear–Fiction, here's what he wrote:

- Fact: "I have a review today."
- Fear: "She might think I'm not good enough."
- Fiction: "I'm going to get fired."

Walking in, he repeated to himself: *"Fact only: I have a review today."* The meeting turned out fine—his boss even complimented his progress.

Reframing didn't just calm Kevin—it gave him the confidence to be present.

The Balanced Voice

Another reframing technique is cultivating your **balanced voice.**

Ask yourself: *If my best friend said this thought out loud, how would I respond?*

If your friend said: *"I completely embarrassed myself. Everyone thinks I'm an idiot,"* would you agree? Of course not. You'd say: *"You're human. Everyone makes mistakes. This doesn't define you."*

Why not speak to yourself the same way?

The balanced voice is not about sugarcoating. It's about fairness. It's giving yourself the compassion you'd give anyone else.

Awareness + Reframing = Calm

Remember Sarah from Chapter Four, who named her spiral during meetings? She took it further by asking herself: *"Is this fact, fear, or fiction?"* Over time, she realized most of her spirals were 90% fiction.

That insight changed everything. She still noticed spirals, but now she had power over them. Awareness gave her space. Reframing shifted her lens. Together, they quieted the spiral.

Guided Practice in Your Journal: Reframe in Writing

1. Write down a spiraling thought.
2. Example: *"I'll fail this project and lose my job."*
3. Draw three columns: Fact | Fear | Fiction.
4. Sort the thought into each.

- Fact: "I have a project due."
- Fear: "I might mess up."
- Fiction: "My boss is waiting for me to fail."

Rewrite the thought in a balanced way.

- *"This project matters, but one assignment doesn't define my career. I can do my best and ask for help if needed."*

Do this once a day for a week. You'll start noticing distortions faster in real time.

Story: Maria and the Party

Maria often spiraled before social events. She worried about what to wear, what to say, how people would judge her. The night before her friend's party, she caught herself thinking: *"Everyone will notice if I say something awkward."*

Using her balanced voice, she reframed: *"People are more focused on themselves than on me. If I'm kind and present, that's what matters."*

The next day, she went—and actually had fun. The spiral didn't vanish, but it no longer controlled her.

Reflection: Shifting the Lens

Think of one recurring thought you've had recently. Maybe about work, relationships, or your own abilities.

Now ask:

- What is the fact?
- What is fear speaking?
- What is pure fiction?
- How can I rewrite this thought more fairly?

Write your answer. Read it aloud. Notice the difference in how it feels.

Key Takeaway

Overthinking thrives on distorted stories. By shifting your lens—asking Fact, Fear, or Fiction—you reframe worry into perspective. Awareness shows you the spiral; reframing changes the way you walk through it.

In the next chapter, we'll explore how calming the body can quiet the mind— because sometimes the fastest way to stop the spiral isn't thinking differently, but **breathing differently.**

Quiet the Body, Quiet the Mind

Have you ever noticed how your thoughts speed up when your heart races? Or how worries feel louder when your shoulders are tense and your breath is shallow? That's because your body and mind are not separate—they're dance partners. When one moves, the other follows.

If you want to calm your mind, one of the fastest ways is to start with your body.

The Mind–Body Connection

When anxiety grips you, your nervous system activates the **fight-or-flight response**. This is an ancient survival mechanism designed to keep humans alive in dangerous situations. Your heart pumps faster to deliver blood to your muscles. Your breath quickens to supply oxygen. Your body tenses, preparing to run or fight.

It's a brilliant system when you're facing a tiger. But in modern life, the "tiger" is usually an email from your boss, an awkward silence, or an unpaid bill.

Your body doesn't know the difference. It reacts as if your life is in danger. And once your body is in alarm mode, your mind scrambles to explain it. *Why is my chest tight? Why is my heart pounding? Something must be wrong. I'd better figure it out.* That, right there, is the spiral in motion.

The Feedback Loop

The relationship between body and mind is a loop:

1. **Trigger:** Something stressful happens.
2. **Body reacts:** Heart races, muscles tense, adrenaline surges.
3. **Mind interprets:** Thoughts spiral to explain the sensations.
4. **Spiral fuels body:** Worries create more adrenaline.
5. **Loop continues.**

The cycle can feel unbreakable—but the good news is, you can interrupt it at either point. You don't always have to "think" your way out. Sometimes, calming your body is the fastest reset button for your mind.

The Body as a Brake Pedal

Think of your nervous system like a car. Anxiety slams on the gas—everything speeds up. Your heart races, your breath shortens, your thoughts scatter.

But you also have a built-in brake pedal: the **parasympathetic nervous system**—often called the "rest-and-digest" system. When activated, it slows your heart, deepens your breath, and calms your body.

The key is learning how to press that brake pedal on purpose.

Practices to Quiet the Body

Here are several proven ways to calm the body and, in turn, quiet the mind.

1. Box Breathing

Used by Navy SEALs to stay calm under pressure.

- Inhale through your nose for a count of four.
- Hold for four.
- Exhale for four.
- Hold for four.
- Repeat for four rounds.

This pattern regulates your nervous system and signals safety to your brain.

2. Progressive Muscle Relaxation

When spiraling, your body is often clenched without you realizing it.

- Starting at your toes, tense your muscles for five seconds, then release.
- Move slowly upward: calves, thighs, stomach, arms, shoulders, face.
- Notice the difference between tension and release.

This practice teaches your body the feeling of letting go.

3. Breath Lengthening

When your exhale is longer than your inhale, your body naturally relaxes. Try inhaling for four counts and exhaling for six.

4. Cold Splash Reset

Splash cold water on your face or hold an ice cube in your hand. This stimulates the vagus nerve, a key player in calming the nervous system.

5. Grounding Movement

Do a few stretches, take a brisk walk, or even shake out your hands. Movement helps burn off the excess adrenaline fueling your spiral.

Story: Mia and the Deadline

Mia was a marketing executive who spiraled before every project deadline. Her chest would tighten, her thoughts would race: *What if I miss something? What if I fail? What if I let everyone down?*

One afternoon, as she felt the spiral building, she tried box breathing. Inhale four, hold four, exhale four, hold four. Within minutes, her body softened. Her shoulders dropped, her chest opened. Her mind still had anxious thoughts—but they felt less urgent.

By calming her body, Mia created space in her mind to focus. She finished her project not in panic, but in steady clarity.

Why Calming the Body Works

When you activate the parasympathetic system, you're telling your brain: *It's safe to relax.* And when the body feels safe, the mind no longer needs to spin endless "what ifs."

It's like quieting an alarm. The spiral doesn't need to search for danger if the siren has been silenced.

A Daily 5-Minute Reset

Here's a simple practice you can use anytime:

1. Sit comfortably with your feet on the ground.

2. Close your eyes and take three slow breaths.
3. Inhale for four, exhale for six—five times.
4. Roll your shoulders back and unclench your jaw.
5. Place a hand on your chest and notice the rhythm of your heartbeat.

In just five minutes, you've pressed the brake pedal.

Exercise: Find Your Reset

Over the next week, experiment with the practices above. Each time you feel a spiral building, try one. Then, in your journal, jot down:

- Which practice you used.
- How your body felt before and after.
- How your thoughts shifted.

By the end of the week, you'll know which reset works best for you. That becomes part of your personal Spiral Toolkit.

Reflection: Your Body as an Ally

For many overthinkers, the body feels like part of the problem. *Why is my heart racing? Why can't I calm down?* But your body is not your enemy. It's your ally. With the right tools, you can use it to step out of spirals faster than thinking ever could.

Key Takeaway

Your body is not just a victim of overthinking—it's also a powerful tool for stopping it. By pressing the brake pedal of the nervous system with breathing, relaxation, or movement, you quiet the body and the mind follows.

In the next chapter, we'll explore another powerful spiral breaker: action.

Because sometimes, the best way to stop the loop is not by thinking less, but by **doing more.**

Stop the Loop with Action

When you're caught in a spiral, your instinct is usually to think your way out of it. *If I just analyze this enough... if I consider every angle... if I replay it one more time, maybe I'll finally feel better.*

But the spiral never delivers on that promise. The more you think, the deeper you sink.

The real escape often comes not from thinking harder—but from doing something, anything, outside the loop.

Why Action Works

Overthinking thrives in stillness. When your body is frozen, your brain has all the space in the world to spin. But when you move into action, you redirect your energy.

Here's the science: taking action engages different brain networks than spiraling. While worry activates the brain's "default mode network" (the system responsible for self-focused rumination), movement and tasks engage the "task-positive network," which pulls your attention outward. In other words, doing shifts your brain out of worry mode.

Action is like changing the channel. You don't have to argue with the spiral—you just stop watching.

42

The Power of Small Steps

The beauty of action is that it doesn't have to be big. You don't need to overhaul your life or solve everything at once. In fact, **the smaller the step, the more powerful it can be.**

Why? Because when you're spiraling, everything feels overwhelming. Taking one tiny step breaks paralysis. It tells your brain: *I'm not stuck. I'm moving forward.* That momentum is often enough to shrink the spiral's grip.

The Two-Minute Shift

One of the simplest action-based strategies is what I call the **Two-Minute Shift.**

Here's how it works:

1. The moment you notice a spiral, commit to doing something— anything—for just two minutes.
2. It doesn't matter what it is: folding laundry, walking outside, washing a dish, sending a quick email.
3. The goal isn't to solve the spiral—it's to interrupt it.

Two minutes feels doable even when you're stuck. And once you start, momentum often carries you further.

Story: Mark and the Midnight Text

Mark was a college student who described himself as "paralyzed by decisions." One night he stayed up until 3 a.m., spiraling over whether to text someone he liked. His thoughts ping-ponged: *Too soon. Too late. Too many emojis. Not enough.*

Finally, out of frustration, he tried something different. He stood up, drank a glass of water, and walked slowly around his apartment. The physical shift broke the loop. His heart slowed. His mind softened. He typed the text, sent it, and—surprise—it was no big deal.

Mark learned that night: the spiral feeds on inaction. The moment you move, you cut off its fuel.

What Action Can Look Like

Action doesn't need to be dramatic. Here are simple ways to interrupt spirals:

- **Move your body:** Take a brisk walk, stretch, dance to one song.
- **Do a quick task:** Load the dishwasher, water a plant, send one email.
- **Connect:** Text a supportive friend, pet your dog, hug your child.
- **Shift focus:** Read a page of a book, listen to music, draw a doodle.
- **Use your senses:** Light a candle, sip tea slowly, splash water on your face.

Notice that none of these involve solving the problem you're spiraling about. The goal is to change your state, not the situation.

Action Creates Clarity

Ironically, many of the decisions you spiral over become clearer once you stop analyzing and start doing.

Think of a time you hesitated endlessly about starting a project. The spiral said: *What if I fail? What if it's not perfect?* But once you actually started— opened the document, sketched the idea—the fear lost power. Action gave you clarity that thinking never could.

It's like fog on a windshield. No amount of staring clears it. You have to turn on the wipers.

Story: Elaine and the Job Search

Elaine lost her job unexpectedly. Every day she sat at her laptop, spiraling: *What if no one hires me? What if I'm not qualified? What if I'm falling behind?*

Her therapist suggested a simple rule: "Send one application a day. Just one."

The first day, she barely managed it. The second day, it felt easier. By the end of the month, she had sent thirty. Two weeks later, she landed interviews.

Action didn't erase her fears. But it gave her something stronger: momentum.

Exercise: Build Your Spiral Interrupter List

Grab your journal. Write down at least ten actions you could take the next time you feel yourself spiraling. Keep them simple and specific.

Examples:

1. Step outside and feel the air.
2. Stretch arms overhead.
3. Drink water slowly.
4. Text a friend and ask how *they're* doing.
5. Play a favorite song and sing along.
6. Write down the spiraling thought, then set the paper aside.
7. Do ten squats or jumping jacks.
8. Wash one dish.
9. Light a candle and watch the flame.
10. Walk around the block.

Keep this list somewhere visible. When the spiral starts, you won't have to think—you'll just pick one and do it.

The Myth of "Motivation"

Many people wait to feel motivated before they act. But motivation doesn't come first—action does. Motivation follows action, not the other way around.

Think about exercise. You rarely feel like starting. But once you do, you often find energy you didn't know you had. The same is true for breaking spirals. The hardest part is beginning.

Reflection: Your Last Spiral

Think back to your last spiral. Imagine if, instead of replaying it for an hour, you had taken two minutes to move, breathe, or do a task. How might it have changed the experience?

Key Takeaway

Overthinking thrives in stillness. Action interrupts the spiral by shifting your energy into motion. Even two minutes of doing—whether moving your body, completing a task, or connecting with someone—can break the loop and restore clarity.

In the next chapter, we'll build on this momentum by decluttering your mental space—simplifying thoughts, routines, and decisions so spirals don't get so much room to grow.

Declutter Your Mental Space

Imagine walking into a room filled with piles of laundry, stacks of papers, half-finished projects, and no clear place to sit. How would you feel? Overwhelmed. Scattered. Stuck.

Now imagine your mind as that room. Thoughts scattered everywhere, to-do lists half-written, worries piled high. It's no wonder overthinking finds so much room to thrive.

Overthinking doesn't happen in a vacuum—it feeds on clutter. The more mental noise you carry, the easier it is for spirals to take root.

This chapter is about clearing that clutter. By simplifying decisions, creating systems, and setting boundaries, you free up mental space—and with it, peace.

Why Overthinking Loves Clutter

Spirals often begin when your mind is overloaded. The brain can only juggle so much information before it tips into overwhelm. Psychologists call this **cognitive load**—the total amount of mental effort being used in working memory.

When your cognitive load is maxed out, two things happen:

1. Small decisions feel monumental.

2. Spirals multiply, filling the space where clarity should be.

Add in the brain's natural **negativity bias**, and suddenly, clutter becomes a breeding ground for worry.

Decision Fatigue: The Hidden Drain

Every day, you make hundreds of decisions—what to wear, what to eat, when to respond, how to spend your time. Even small choices add up.

Researchers call this **decision fatigue.** By the end of the day, your mental fuel tank is empty. That's when you're most likely to spiral: late at night, staring at the ceiling, too drained to think clearly but unable to stop thinking.

Think about it: Do you spiral more often at 9 a.m. or 11 p.m.? For most people, spirals thrive in exhaustion.

Simplifying to Create Space

One of the most powerful ways to fight overthinking is to reduce the number of decisions you have to make. The less clutter in your mental room, the less fuel for spirals.

1. Automate the Small Stuff

- Eat the same breakfast each morning.
- Set bills to auto-pay.
- Use reminders for recurring tasks.
- When small choices are automated, your mind has more space for what matters.

2. Batch Decisions

Instead of deciding meals or outfits every day, plan them weekly. Instead of answering emails constantly, check at set times. Batching reduces decision fatigue and creates rhythm.

3. Write It Down

Stop carrying everything in your head. Keep a running list—tasks, ideas, reminders—on paper or in an app. Your brain is for creating, not storing.

4. Limit Inputs

Too much information is mental clutter. Be intentional about what you consume: fewer news alerts, fewer social media scrolls, fewer opinions pulling at you.

Story: Jenna's To-Do List Overload

Jenna, a teacher, described her mind as "a hundred browser tabs open at once." She carried lesson plans, grading, student struggles, bills, and family concerns in her head all at once.

By bedtime, her mind felt like a storm. She couldn't fall asleep because every unfinished task replayed.

When she tried the **one-minute brain dump**—writing down everything in her head without editing—she was shocked by how light she felt. "It's like closing all the tabs," she said. "I can finally breathe."

The tasks hadn't disappeared. But the clutter had moved from her head to paper, and that shift gave her peace.

The One-Minute Brain Dump

Here's how it works:

1. Set a timer for one minute.
2. Write down everything swirling in your head: tasks, worries, reminders, random thoughts. Don't edit or organize—just dump.
3. When the timer stops, look at the list. Circle what actually matters today. Cross out what doesn't.

This simple exercise clears mental clutter. You don't have to hold everything in your head at once.

The Worry Window

Another tool for decluttering mental space is creating a **worry window.**

Instead of letting worry hijack your day, you set aside a specific 15-minute block for it.

- During the day, when a worry pops up, tell yourself: *"Not now—I'll think about it during my window."*
- At your set time, sit down and let yourself write out or reflect on your worries.
- When the timer ends, close the window and move on.

This creates boundaries for worry instead of letting it sprawl across your entire life.

Story: Amir and the Midnight Spiral

Amir often spiraled at night, lying awake for hours with "what if" scenarios. He began scheduling his worry window right after dinner. He would sit down, set a timer, and pour all his fears onto paper.

At first, it felt silly. But soon, his midnight spirals shrank. His brain learned: *Worry has a time and place. It doesn't belong in bed.*

Exercise: Declutter Your Day

Tonight, try this:

1. Do a one-minute brain dump.
2. Circle one thing you can act on tomorrow.
3. Cross out one thing that doesn't actually matter.
4. Place the paper aside and give yourself permission to rest.

Over time, this ritual tells your mind: *I'm in charge of my mental space.*

Reflection: The Cost of Clutter

Ask yourself:

- What's one area of my life where too many choices overwhelm me?
- What could I automate, batch, or simplify?
- How would my spiral change if my mental "room" was clearer?

Write your answers in your journal. Simplification isn't laziness—it's wisdom.

Key Takeaway

Overthinking thrives in mental clutter. By simplifying routines, limiting decisions, and setting boundaries for worry, you create space for peace to grow.

In the next chapter, we'll take this further—learning how to set **boundaries with your thoughts** so they stop barging in and taking over your mental space.

Boundaries with Your Thoughts

Not every thought that enters your mind deserves your full attention.

But if you're an overthinker, it feels like they do. Each thought arrives with urgency, waving its arms: *What if this matters? What if this is true? What if you ignore me and regret it forever?*

So you stop, you listen, you analyze. Before long, you're tangled in thoughts that never earned the right to control your energy in the first place.

This chapter is about building mental boundaries. Just as you wouldn't let a stranger walk into your home and take over, you don't have to let every thought move in and rearrange the furniture.

You Are Not Your Thoughts

One of the most liberating truths you can learn is this: **you are not your thoughts.**

Thoughts are mental events—stories, guesses, fears, memories, plans. Some are helpful. Some are not. But they are not you.

Think of thoughts like clouds passing across the sky. The sky doesn't chase or fight the clouds. It simply holds space for them. You are the sky. Your thoughts are the clouds.

When you remember this, you stop identifying with every single thought as if it defines you.

Cognitive Fusion vs. Defusion

Psychologists use the term **cognitive fusion** to describe what happens when we're stuck to our thoughts. In fusion, thoughts feel like absolute truth: *I'm a failure. I'll never get this right. Everyone thinks I'm annoying.*

Cognitive defusion is the skill of stepping back and seeing thoughts as thoughts. Instead of *"I'm a failure,"* you notice: *"I'm having the thought that I'm a failure."* That tiny shift creates distance.

It's the difference between being trapped inside a storm and watching the storm pass through.

Metaphors for Setting Boundaries

Sometimes metaphors help us "see" the process more clearly:

- **Leaves on a Stream:** Picture each thought as a leaf floating down a river. You don't grab them; you watch them drift by.
- **Passengers on a Bus:** You're the driver. Thoughts are passengers shouting directions. Some are loud, some rude, some helpful. You hear them, but you decide the route.
- **Pop-Up Ads:** Thoughts are like internet pop-ups. Just because they appear on your screen doesn't mean you have to click.

These metaphors remind you: thoughts are not commands. You get to choose which ones deserve attention.

Story: Daniel and His Inner Critic

Daniel struggled with self-criticism. After every mistake, his mind screamed: *"You're useless. You'll never succeed."* He fused with those thoughts, believing they reflected who he was.

Then he learned defusion. Each time the critic appeared, he said: *"I notice I'm having the thought that I'm useless."* At first, it felt clunky. But slowly, the critic's words lost their bite.

They became background noise rather than defining truth.

Daniel realized: the thoughts hadn't disappeared. But their power over him had.

The Practice of Labeling

Here's a simple way to set boundaries: **label your thoughts.**

Instead of saying: *"I'm going to fail,"* shift to: *"I'm having the thought that I'm going to fail."*

That small phrase—*"I'm having the thought that..."*—creates a gap. The thought moves from fact to observation. You are the observer, not the thought.

The Thought Gate Exercise

Visualize your mind as a garden with a gate. Thoughts arrive like visitors. Some are welcome—helpful, kind, wise. Others are noisy, critical, or draining.

As the gardener, you decide: who gets to enter? Who stays outside the gate?

Each time a thought shows up, imagine greeting it at the gate. Ask: *"Do I want you inside my space?"* If not, kindly let it pass by.

Story: Leah and the Interview Spiral

Leah had an upcoming job interview. Her mind spun: *"I'll say something stupid. They'll hate me. I'll embarrass myself."*

Instead of analyzing, she tried the thought gate. She pictured those thoughts knocking. She smiled politely and said: *"Not today. You don't get to run this interview."*

The thoughts didn't vanish, but they stayed outside. Leah walked into the interview calmer, more grounded.

Boundaries Don't Mean Avoidance

Important note: setting boundaries with thoughts isn't about denial or suppression. It's about discernment. Some thoughts deserve your energy— like problem-solving a real challenge. Others are noise, fear, or fiction.

Boundaries mean you choose. You stop treating every thought like an urgent command.

Practice: Thought Journaling

For the next three days, use your journal. Each time a spiral starts:

1. Write down one dominant thought.
2. Prefix it with: *"I'm noticing the thought that..."*
3. Ask: Does this thought deserve my energy right now?
4. If yes, take a small action. If no, let it pass.

Over time, this journal becomes evidence that you are separate from your thoughts.

Reflection: What Boundaries Feel Like

Think of a time you said no to someone who drained you. Remember how freeing it felt to protect your energy? Setting boundaries with thoughts works the same way.

Ask yourself:

- Which recurring thought in my life needs a boundary?
- How might my day change if I stopped giving it power?

Key Takeaway

Thoughts are not facts, commands, or prophecies. They are mental events. By setting boundaries—through labeling, metaphors, or the thought gate— you reclaim authority. You stop absorbing every thought as truth and start choosing which ones deserve your attention.

In the next chapter, we'll build on this by reclaiming your inner voice— transforming self-criticism into self-compassion.

Reclaim Your Inner Voice

If overthinking had a soundtrack, it would often be narrated by your own voice—only harsher.

It says things like:
"You always screw things up."
"Why can't you get it right?"
"Everyone's judging you."

This is the **inner critic** at work. It means well, in its twisted way—it's trying to protect you from mistakes, embarrassment, or rejection. But instead of helping, it magnifies fear. And when your own mind becomes hostile territory, spirals tighten even faster.

But here's the good news: your inner voice is not fixed. It can shift from critic to coach, from enemy to ally. And that shift may be the most powerful spiral breaker of all.

The Damage of Self-Criticism

Self-criticism fuels overthinking in two major ways:

1. **It keeps the loop alive.** Harsh thoughts replay endlessly, convincing you to analyze every flaw and failure.
2. **It erodes confidence.** The more you criticize yourself, the less you

trust your judgment—so you second-guess every decision.

Over time, this doesn't just affect how you think—it affects how you live. You avoid risks, shrink back from opportunities, and live cautiously instead of fully.

Why We Listen to the Critic

If the inner critic is so painful, why do we keep listening to it?

Psychologists suggest it often comes from childhood experiences. Maybe you internalized critical parents, demanding teachers, or comparisons to siblings. Or maybe perfectionism grew out of praise only for achievements, not for effort.

The critic becomes a "familiar voice." And familiar feels safe—even when it's harmful.

But safe and true are not the same thing.

The Power of Self-Compassion

Research led by Dr. Kristin Neff shows that people who practice **self-compassion**—treating themselves with the same kindness they'd offer a friend—are less anxious, less depressed, and more resilient.

Self-compassion doesn't mean letting yourself off the hook. It means responding to mistakes and struggles with understanding instead of attack.

Think of it this way: If your best friend told you, *"I bombed that presentation. I'm terrible at my job,"* would you reply, *"You're right, you're awful"*? Of course not. You'd say, *"It was one presentation. You care about your work, and you'll do better next time."*

Why not offer yourself the same grace?

Story: Maya the Perfectionist

Maya was a high-achieving law student whose inner critic was relentless. Every exam, every paper, every internship review triggered spirals. Her critic said: *"You'll never be enough. Everyone else is smarter."*

When she began practicing self-compassion, it felt fake at first. But over time, she reframed her thoughts:

- From *"I'll never be enough"* → *"I'm learning, just like everyone else."*
- From *"Everyone else is smarter"* → *"I bring my own strengths to the table."*

Her critic still spoke, but now she had another voice—one that soothed instead of scolded. The spiral loosened.

Reframing the Inner Voice

Here's a simple practice:

1. Write down one critical thought you often hear.
2. Example: *"I'm such an idiot for forgetting that deadline."*
3. Rewrite it as if you were speaking to a friend.
4. Example: *"Deadlines are tough. You had a lot on your plate. Next time, you'll set a reminder."*
5. Read the compassionate version aloud.

Notice the difference in your body. The critic tightens. Compassion softens.

The Three Pillars of Self-Compassion

According to Dr. Neff, self-compassion rests on three pillars:

1. **Self-Kindness vs. Self-Judgment**
2. Speak to yourself with understanding, not attack.
3. **Common Humanity vs. Isolation**
4. Remember that mistakes and struggles are part of being human—not proof of your inadequacy.
5. **Mindfulness vs. Over-Identification**
6. Notice your pain without exaggerating it. Instead of *"This is the end,"* remind yourself, *"This is hard, and it will pass."*

Practicing these three shifts rewires how you speak to yourself.

Exercise: The Compassionate Letter

Try writing a short letter to yourself as if you were writing to someone you deeply care about.

Include:

- Acknowledge the struggle: *"I know you're worried about failing this project."*
- Offer understanding: *"It makes sense you feel anxious—you care about doing well."*
- Remind yourself of strengths: *"You've handled challenges before and you'll handle this one too."*
- Close with encouragement: *"You're learning, you're growing, and you are enough."*

Keep the letter. Reread it when the critic grows loud.

Story: Javier and the Critic's Echo

Javier grew up with a father who demanded perfection. As an adult, he found himself echoing the same tone in his own head. After a single mistake at work, his spiral screamed: *"You'll never be good enough."*

When he learned self-compassion practices, he started pausing to ask: *"Would I say this to someone I love?"* The answer was always no. Slowly, he rewrote the script. His critic's echo grew quieter.

Practice: Compassionate Breath

Each time you catch a critical thought, try this:

1. Place a hand over your heart.
2. Take a slow breath in and out.
3. Whisper a compassionate phrase:

- *"I'm doing the best I can."*
- *"This moment is hard, but I can meet it with kindness."*
- *"I am learning, and that's enough."*

This simple act activates your body's calming system and pairs it with a new voice.

Reflection: Your Ally Within

Think of a time someone spoke kindly to you when you were struggling. How did it feel? Now imagine carrying that same voice inside your head—not as an exception, but as a daily companion.

That is the voice you're reclaiming.

Key Takeaway

Overthinking thrives on self-criticism. By shifting from critic to compassion, you soften spirals and rebuild trust in yourself. Self-compassion is not indulgence—it's strength. It gives you the courage to act, the clarity to decide, and the peace to rest.

In the next chapter, we'll take compassion out into the world—bringing mindfulness into motion so peace becomes part of your everyday rhythm.

Peace in Motion

When most people hear the word *mindfulness,* they picture someone sitting cross-legged in silence, breathing slowly, maybe even chanting. And while meditation is one form of mindfulness, it's not the only one.

The truth is, you don't need to sit still on a cushion to practice mindfulness. You can carry it with you as you walk, eat, work, talk, and listen.

Peace isn't something you visit in rare, quiet moments. It's something you can learn to live inside of—even while life keeps moving.

Why Everyday Mindfulness Matters

Overthinking thrives when your mind wanders into the past or the future. It replays what you said, predicts what might go wrong, analyzes what you should have done differently. Mindfulness interrupts that pattern by anchoring you in the present.

Think of mindfulness as the opposite of spiraling.

- Spiraling pulls you away from the present.
- Mindfulness pulls you back into it.

And when practiced in everyday life, mindfulness becomes sustainable. Instead of waiting for a vacation or a meditation session to feel calm, you weave calm into your daily rhythm.

The Anchor Effect

When anxiety and spirals take over, it feels like being swept up in a storm. Everyday mindfulness gives you anchors—small, repeatable practices that tether you to the here and now.

- A deep breath before opening your inbox.
- Paying attention to the taste of your coffee instead of scrolling.
- Listening fully when someone speaks, instead of rehearsing your reply.

These moments might seem small, but they accumulate. Over time, they train your brain to return to calm more quickly.

Story: Alex's Commute

Alex dreaded his daily commute. Traffic gave him plenty of time to replay every mistake at work and rehearse every possible disaster. By the time he arrived, he was already drained.

One morning, he tried something different. He turned off the radio and focused on his senses: the feel of the steering wheel, the rhythm of his breath, the sights outside his window. Each time his mind wandered, he gently returned to those anchors.

He described the change this way: *"Instead of arriving already exhausted, I started arriving steady. The drive didn't change. I did."*

Everyday Opportunities for Peace

Mindfulness doesn't require extra time—you can practice it inside the life you already live.

Walking

Instead of spiraling while you walk, notice the rhythm of your steps, the pressure of your feet on the ground, the movement of your arms. Feel the air against your skin.

Eating

Slow down at meals. Notice the colors, textures, and flavors. Put down your phone and let eating itself be an experience, not just a task.

Listening

When talking to someone, notice their tone, their expressions, their pauses. Listen without rehearsing your response. Presence deepens connection.

Waiting

Lines, red lights, or hold music are common spiral zones. Instead of fuming, practice awareness: breathe, look around, notice three things you can see, hear, and feel.

Micro-Mindfulness

Even thirty seconds of attention can reset your mind. Try these micro-practices:

- Take one slow breath before answering the phone.

- Sip tea or water and notice its temperature and texture.
- Stretch your arms overhead and notice the release.
- Step outside for a moment and feel the air.

Tiny practices, repeated often, rewire the brain.

The Science of Presence

Studies show that mindfulness practices increase activity in the prefrontal cortex (responsible for focus and decision-making) and decrease activity in the amygdala (the brain's fear center). Regular mindfulness doesn't just calm spirals in the moment—it makes your brain more resilient over time.

Even short, frequent practices matter more than rare, long ones. Five mindful breaths scattered through your day may benefit you more than a once-a-week meditation.

Story: Hannah and the Dinner Table

Hannah was a mother of three who felt constantly distracted. At dinner, her body was at the table, but her mind was elsewhere—rehashing the day or planning tomorrow.

One evening, she challenged herself to stay fully present for the meal. She noticed the crunch of lettuce, the laughter of her kids, the warmth of her husband's hand brushing hers.

Later, she realized she couldn't remember the last time she had actually *tasted* her food or *heard* her children's voices without distraction. That night sparked a change: she began treating meals as mindfulness practice. The spiral had one less foothold.

Exercise: Choose Your Anchor

Pick one daily activity you already do—making coffee, brushing your teeth, walking the dog. Decide that this activity will be your **mindful anchor.**

Each time you do it:

1. Slow down.
2. Pay attention to your senses—what you see, hear, feel, smell, or taste.
3. If your mind wanders, gently return to the activity.

Practice this for one week. Notice how your spiral shifts when you make mindfulness a habit woven into life instead of a separate chore.

Beyond Calm: Connection and Joy

Everyday mindfulness doesn't just reduce spirals—it expands joy. When you're fully present, you notice more beauty, connection, and meaning.

- A smile from a stranger.
- The way sunlight falls across your desk.
- A moment of laughter that would have slipped by unnoticed.

Overthinking robs you of these moments. Mindfulness gives them back.

Reflection: A Day Lived Fully

Imagine living one full day where every ordinary activity becomes a mindful one. You wake up and stretch, feeling your body instead of reaching for your phone. You savor your breakfast. You walk outside and notice the world. You listen deeply when people speak. You fall asleep not with spirals, **but with gratitude**.

That life isn't far away. It begins with a single mindful moment.

Key Takeaway

Mindfulness isn't limited to meditation. It's a way of moving through life—anchoring yourself in ordinary moments so spirals have less power. By carrying peace into motion, you create calm that lasts.

In the next chapter, we'll prepare for the storms—building **resilience in stressful times** so spirals don't sweep you away when life gets messy.

Resilience in Stressful Times

Life will never stop handing us challenges. Jobs change. Relationships shift. Health scares arrive. Plans fall apart. Stressful times are not optional—they're guaranteed.

But spiraling in response to them? That's optional.

Resilience is what allows you to bend without breaking. It's the skill that helps you feel the weight of life without collapsing under it. And while some people seem "naturally resilient," the truth is resilience is not a personality trait—it's a practice. One you can strengthen like a muscle.

What Resilience Really Is

Resilience isn't pretending everything is fine. It isn't about suppressing emotions or forcing yourself to "just be positive."

Resilience means you experience stress, but you recover more quickly. You face challenges with flexibility instead of rigidity, with perspective instead of panic.

Think of a tree in the wind. A brittle tree snaps under pressure. A flexible tree bends, sways, and eventually stands upright again. Resilience is that flexibility.

The Spiral vs. Resilience

When something stressful happens, the spiral says:

- *"This is the end. I'll never recover."*
- *"Everything is ruined."*
- *"I can't handle this."*

Resilience says:

- *"This is hard, but it's temporary."*
- *"Things didn't go as planned, but I can adapt."*
- *"I've survived challenges before. I'll survive this too."*

Both voices may show up. But resilience is the one you choose to amplify.

The Physiology of Resilience

Resilience has roots in the nervous system. People who recover quickly from stress show a strong **parasympathetic rebound**—their bodies shift out of fight-or-flight faster.

That's why practices like breathing, grounding, and mindfulness are not just "nice ideas"—they physically train your nervous system to reset. The more often you practice, the quicker your recovery in real storms.

Story: Emily's Job Loss

Emily lost her job without warning. Her spiral screamed: *"I'll never find another. I can't afford this. Everything is falling apart."* Her body buzzed with panic.

But she paused, took a breath, and reminded herself: *"This is hard, but I've faced hard before."*

Next, she pivoted to what she could control: updating her résumé, reaching out to her network, reviewing her budget. Finally, she proceeded by sending one application that very day.

Within weeks, she found a new job—one she ended up enjoying more.

Emily didn't erase her stress. She built resilience in the middle of it.

The Pause–Pivot–Proceed Method

Here's a simple framework for resilience:

1. **Pause.** When stress hits, take one slow breath. This interrupts automatic spirals.
2. **Pivot.** Ask: *"What's in my control right now?"* Focus on that—not the thousand things outside your control.
3. **Proceed.** Take one small step forward. Send the email. Make the call. Take the walk.

This method transforms overwhelm into manageable action.

Why Resilience Feels Empowering

When spirals take over, you feel powerless—like life is happening *to* you. Resilience restores your sense of agency. It doesn't promise ease, but it gives you choices. And choices are empowering.

Story: Darren and the Divorce

Darren described his divorce as "the darkest storm" of his life. He could have spiraled for years in bitterness. Instead, he practiced small resilience steps. Each morning, he asked: *"What's one thing I can do today to care for myself?"* Sometimes it was cooking a meal.

Sometimes it was calling a friend. Sometimes it was just walking outside.

Months later, he looked back and realized those tiny steps had carried him through. He hadn't avoided pain, but he hadn't drowned in it either.

Exercise: Resilience Reflection

Think back to a challenge you've faced before. Write down:

- What happened.
- How you got through it.
- What strengths you discovered in yourself.

This reflection proves something vital: you've already been resilient. The evidence is in your past. And if you did it then, you can do it again.

Building Everyday Resilience

Resilience isn't built only in big storms—it's trained in small ones. Every time you:

- Pause before reacting in anger.
- Take a breath instead of spiraling.
- Show yourself compassion after a mistake.
- Reframe a setback as temporary.

You're building micro-resilience. These small practices prepare you for larger challenges.

Practical Habits That Grow Resilience

1. **Daily grounding.** Even 5 minutes of breathwork or mindfulness trains your nervous system.
2. **Movement.** Exercise builds both physical and emotional stamina.
3. **Connection.** Talking with trusted people prevents isolation—the spiral's favorite fuel.
4. **Journaling.** Writing about stress helps you process instead of overthink.
5. **Rest.** Sleep is resilience training. Exhaustion makes everything harder.

Reflection: Your Personal Resilience Plan

Ask yourself:

- What small daily practice could strengthen my resilience?
- Who are the people I can reach out to when storms hit?
- What past victories remind me I can handle hard things?

Write your answers. This becomes your personal resilience plan.

Key Takeaway

Resilience doesn't mean avoiding stress. It means facing it with flexibility, perspective, and action. By pausing, pivoting to what you can control, and proceeding with one small step, you build the strength to withstand storms without spiraling.

In the next (and final) chapter, we'll bring everything together—showing how a quiet mind leads not to passivity, but to boldness, clarity, and joy.

Gratitude as a Grounding Practice

When spirals take over, your mind races toward what's missing, what's uncertain, or what could go wrong. Gratitude pulls you in the opposite direction. It points you to what is steady, present, and already good.

Gratitude is not about ignoring pain or pretending everything is fine. It's about balance. It's about widening your view so anxiety isn't the only voice in the room.

In the middle of a storm, gratitude is like a flashlight. It doesn't erase the darkness, but it gives you something steady to hold onto.

Why Gratitude Works Against Spirals

Overthinking thrives on scarcity and fear. *I don't have enough time. I don't have enough ability. What if I lose what I have?*

Gratitude interrupts that loop by shifting your focus from lack to presence. Instead of circling what's missing, you notice what's here.

Research supports this. Studies show that people who practice gratitude regularly report lower anxiety, improved sleep, better relationships, and greater resilience. Gratitude doesn't just change how you feel—it changes how your brain operates.

The Science of Gratitude

Neuroscientists have found that gratitude activates the brain's **dopamine and serotonin systems**—the same networks associated with reward and contentment. Over time, this rewires your brain to notice more positives automatically.

Think of it like training a muscle. The more you practice gratitude, the stronger your "positivity filter" becomes. Spirals may still show up, but gratitude makes them less sticky.

Gratitude in Motion

Gratitude is most powerful when paired with mindfulness. Together, they root you in the present.

- **Mindfulness says:** *I notice what's here.*
- **Gratitude says:** *And I appreciate it.*

This combination transforms ordinary moments into grounding ones.

- Drinking coffee slowly, savoring warmth and flavor.
- Walking outside, noticing sunlight on your face or the sound of birds.
- Listening to laughter and letting yourself smile without analyzing.

Each moment of gratitude is a tether, pulling you out of the spiral and into life as it's happening.

Story: Rachel and the Bedtime Spiral

Rachel often spiraled at night. She replayed conversations, worried about tomorrow's tasks, and lay awake for hours. One evening, she tried something new. Instead of spiraling, she grabbed a notebook and wrote down three things she was grateful for:

1. A coworker who helped her finish a project.
2. The taste of warm soup she had for dinner.
3. The way her dog curled up beside her.

At first, it felt forced. But after a few nights, she noticed a shift. Her mind calmed more quickly, and sleep came easier. Gratitude didn't erase her worries, but it softened them enough to let her rest.

The Three Blessings Practice

One of the simplest gratitude exercises is called **Three Blessings.** Each night, before bed:

1. Write down three things that went well today.
2. Beside each one, write why it mattered.

- Example: *"Had coffee with a friend—reminded me I'm not alone."*

Over time, this practice reshapes how you end your days. Instead of falling asleep in a spiral of what went wrong, you close the day grounded in what went right.

Gratitude Reframes

Another way to use gratitude as a spiral breaker is to reframe "I have to" into "I get to."

- Spiral: *"I have to go to work tomorrow."*
- Gratitude reframe: *"I get to go to work tomorrow—I have a job and income."*
- Spiral: *"I have to do laundry."*
- Gratitude reframe: *"I get to do laundry—I have clothes to wear."*

- Spiral: *"I have to pick up my kids."*
- Gratitude reframe: *"I get to pick up my kids—I have the privilege of being part of their lives."*

This doesn't mean ignoring frustration. It means balancing frustration with appreciation.

Story: Charles and the Commute

Charles hated his daily commute. Traffic was a spiral trigger—forty minutes of frustration, replaying mistakes or predicting problems at work.

One day, he decided to experiment. Each red light, he named one thing he was grateful for: his reliable car, the podcast he was listening to, the paycheck waiting at the end of the week.

The commute didn't get shorter, but it got lighter. Gratitude transformed wasted time into grounding time.

Exercise: Gratitude Walk

Set aside ten minutes for a walk. As you move, notice and silently name things you appreciate.

- The feel of your feet on the ground.
- The air on your skin.
- A flower blooming, a bird calling, a neighbor's wave.

By the end, you'll feel more present, less tangled in worry. This is gratitude in motion.

Gratitude in Stressful Times

Gratitude isn't just for good days—it's especially powerful in hard ones.

When life feels heavy, gratitude doesn't deny the pain. It simply reminds you that even in difficulty, small pockets of goodness remain.

- Gratitude for a friend who checks in.
- Gratitude for a moment of laughter in grief.
- Gratitude for your own strength in showing up.

This doesn't erase hardship. But it creates balance—enough balance to keep the spiral from consuming everything.

Reflection: Your Gratitude Snapshot

Take a moment right now. Write down three things you're grateful for *today*. Not yesterday, not someday—today. Big or small, it doesn't matter.

Notice how you feel after writing them. Gratitude grounds you in the here and now, one acknowledgment at a time.

Key Takeaway

Gratitude interrupts spirals by shifting focus from what's missing to what's present. It's not denial—it's balance. Practiced daily, gratitude rewires your brain to notice positives, grounds you in mindfulness, and anchors you through storms.

In the next (and final) chapter, we'll bring all the tools together—showing how awareness, reframing, calming the body, action, decluttering, boundaries, compassion, mindfulness, resilience, and gratitude create not just quiet minds, but bold, calm lives.

A Bold, Calm Life

For most of your life, you may have believed the spiral defined you. That the endless loops of "what ifs" and "should haves" were simply part of who you are. That your anxious, overthinking mind was permanent.

But now you know better.

The spiral is not who you are. It's a pattern. A habit. And habits can change.

This final chapter is about stepping into what comes next: not just a quieter mind, but a calmer, bolder life.

Calm Is Not Weakness

Some people fear that if they calm their minds, they'll lose their edge. They think spiraling is what makes them responsible, prepared, or successful.

The truth? Spiraling drains energy without giving results. Calm doesn't make you passive—it makes you powerful.

It's the difference between flailing in quicksand and walking steadily on solid ground. When your mind is clear, you don't second-guess every move. You trust yourself. You act with confidence.

Calm isn't the absence of drive—it's the presence of clarity.

Putting It All Together

Look at the journey you've taken through this book:

- **Awareness** showed you how to pause the spin.
- **Reframing** shifted your lens from fear to perspective.
- **Quieting the body** reminded you that peace often starts below the neck.
- **Action** taught you to interrupt spirals by moving instead of thinking.
- **Decluttering** cleared mental space so spirals had less room to grow.
- **Boundaries with thoughts** gave you authority over your inner world.
- **Compassion** softened the inner critic into an ally.
- **Mindfulness in motion** brought presence into your daily rhythm.
- **Resilience** prepared you to bend without breaking in life's storms.
- **Gratitude** anchored you in what's steady, present, and good.

Each tool is powerful on its own. Together, they form a framework—a way of living where spirals no longer define you.

Story: Olivia's Transformation

Olivia, a nurse, once described herself as "a prisoner of her thoughts." Spirals stole her sleep, drained her joy, and made her question her worth.

Over time, she began applying these tools. She noticed her spirals sooner. She reframed them with fact, fear, and fiction. She used her breath to calm her body, took short walks to reset, and ended her days with gratitude journaling.

Months later, she said: *"My life hasn't gotten easier. But I've gotten calmer. And with that calm, I'm braver than I've ever been."*

That is a bold, calm life. Not a life free of stress, but a life where stress doesn't steal everything.

Boldness Born from Calm

When your spirals no longer control you, you have energy for what truly matters:

- Speaking up in meetings without replaying every word.
- Saying yes to opportunities without drowning in "what ifs."
- Resting at night instead of spinning through worst-case scenarios.
- Being present with loved ones instead of distracted by mental noise.

This is boldness—not recklessness, but the courage to live fully, fueled by calm.

A Spiral-Free Vision of Your Future

Picture yourself one year from now. You still face challenges. You still have responsibilities. Spirals still knock at the door.

But instead of being swept away, you pause. You notice. You breathe. You act. You reframe. You give thanks. You move forward.

Your life feels lighter—not because the world has changed, but because you have.

The Practice of Integration

Living boldly and calmly is not about perfection. You won't use every tool every day. You'll still spiral sometimes.

But each time you practice—even for a moment—you strengthen your new way of living. Think of it like building muscle. A single workout won't transform you. But consistent practice reshapes you over time.

- A single mindful breath.
- A single reframed thought.
- A single act of compassion toward yourself.
- A single gratitude note at bedtime.

These moments accumulate. They change you.

Reflection: Your Spiral Is Not Your Story

Close your eyes for a moment. Place your hand on your chest. Say silently to yourself:

"My spiral is not my story. I am more than my thoughts. I am calm. I am bold."

Let those words settle in. This is your truth now.

Your Next Chapter

The pages of this book are ending. But your next chapter is just beginning.

You've learned how to step outside the spiral, reclaim your energy, and root yourself in calm. Now comes the daily practice of living it.

Every time you pause, reframe, breathe, move, simplify, set boundaries, show compassion, notice the present, bend without breaking, and give thanks—you are writing a new story.

A story not of endless spirals, but of clarity, courage, and joy.

Key Takeaway

A calm mind is not a retreat from life—it's the foundation of a bold one. By quieting the spiral, you don't lose yourself. You find yourself. And from that center, you can live more fully, love more deeply, and step forward with steady confidence.

Final Words

This is your invitation: to stop living as a prisoner of your spirals and start living as the author of your own story.

The spiral may whisper, but now you have the tools to answer it with calm, clarity, and choice.

You don't need to think your way into peace. You can live your way into it—moment by moment, breath by breath.

Your spiral is not your story. Your calm is.

30-Day Spiral Breaker Plan

Here's a simple month-long plan to help you integrate the practices from this book into daily life.

Week 1: Awareness & Reframing

- Day 1: Spiral Spotting — write down 3 spirals you notice.
- Day 2: Name It to Tame It — label your next anxious thought.
- Day 3: Practice the Fact–Fear–Fiction filter.
- Day 4: Balanced Voice journaling — rewrite 1 critic thought.
- Day 5: One 3-minute awareness pause.
- Day 6: Try one "observer seat" metaphor.
- Day 7: Reflect on changes you notice.

Week 2: Body & Action

- Day 8: Practice box breathing.
- Day 9: Do progressive muscle relaxation.
- Day 10: Try a grounding walk.
- Day 11: Two-Minute Shift — interrupt one spiral with action.
- Day 12: Add one "spiral interrupter" to your list.
- Day 13: Do a 5-minute daily reset (breathe, stretch, ground).
- Day 14: Reflect in your journal: How did action change your spirals?

Week 3: Mental Space & Compassion

- Day 15: One-minute brain dump.
- Day 16: Schedule a 15-minute worry window.
- Day 17: Practice "I'm noticing the thought that…" once.
- Day 18: Write a compassionate letter to yourself.
- Day 19: Try the Thought Gate visualization.
- Day 20: Whisper a compassionate breath phrase.
- Day 21: Reflect: Did boundaries change how thoughts felt?

Week 4: Mindfulness, Resilience, Gratitude

- Day 22: Choose 1 mindful anchor (coffee, shower, walk).
- Day 23: Gratitude walk — name 5 things you notice.
- Day 24: Write down 3 blessings before bed.
- Day 25: Practice Pause–Pivot–Proceed once today.
- Day 26: Reframe "I have to" into "I get to."
- Day 27: Write your resilience reflection (past challenge you overcame).
- Day 28: Practice one micro-mindfulness moment (breath, sip, stretch).
- Day 29: Gratitude journaling — what went right today?
- Day 30: Reflection — How does life feel now vs. Day 1?

Emergency Spiral Toolkit

Use this quick-reference list whenever a spiral hits.

- **Pause & Name It:** "This is worry. This is predicting."
- **Breathe:** Box breathing or 4–6 breath lengthening.
- **Move:** Two-minute walk, stretch, or action task.
- **Reframe:** Fact–Fear–Fiction filter.
- **Compassion:** "I'm doing the best I can."
- **Gratitude:** Name one thing that's steady right now.
- **Anchor:** Notice 3 things you can see, 2 you can hear, 1 you can feel.

Conclusion

Your Spiral-Free Future

You began this journey believing the spiral was in control. The racing thoughts, the sleepless nights, the endless loops—they felt like part of who you were.

But now you've learned the truth: the spiral is not you. It's a pattern. And patterns can be broken.

You've discovered how to:

- Pause with **awareness**.
- Reframe with **perspective**.
- Calm your body to quiet your mind.
- Break loops with **action**.
- Simplify and **declutter**.
- Set boundaries with your thoughts.
- Reclaim your inner voice with **compassion**.
- Carry **mindfulness** into everyday life.
- Build **resilience** in stressful times.
- Anchor yourself in **gratitude**.
- Step forward into a **bold, calm life**.

This is not the end of your journey. It's the beginning. A spiral-free future doesn't mean you'll never worry, never overthink, never feel anxious again. It means you'll know what to do when those moments come.

You'll breathe. You'll notice. You'll choose. You'll live.

Your spiral does not define your story. From this moment forward, your calm, bold life begins.

Afterword

If you've made it here, I want you to pause and let that sink in. You chose to open this book, to face the spiral instead of letting it run unchecked, and to take the first steps toward peace.

That alone is powerful.

This book was never about eliminating thoughts. It was about giving you choices. About reminding you that you are bigger than your spiral.

The truth is, overthinking doesn't disappear overnight. Spirals may still show up, whispering the same old fears. But now, you have tools. You have awareness. You have choice. And that changes everything.

Remember—calm doesn't mean a life free of stress. Calm means you meet stress differently. You pause. You breathe. You notice. You act. You give thanks. And little by little, you shape a bold, calm life you once thought was impossible.

So carry this work with you. Return to the practices that resonated most. Scribble in your journal, take your gratitude walks, breathe through the rush of your day. Let these tools become second nature, like anchors scattered across your life.

And on the days when the spiral feels loud again, please remember this: you are not alone, you are not broken, and your spiral is not your story.

Your story is one of strength. Of courage. Of choosing presence over panic, clarity over noise, and boldness over fear.

Step forward with confidence. Your bold, calm life is waiting.

Carry these tools with you. Practice them daily. Return to them when life feels heavy.

And always remember:
You are not your spiral.
You are calm.
You are bold.
You are free.

References

On Overthinking & Anxiety

Clark, D. A., & Beck, A. T. (2011). Cognitive Therapy of Anxiety Disorders.

Leahy, R. L. (2019). The Worry Cure: Seven Steps to Stop Worry from Stopping You.

On Mindfulness & Presence

Kabat-Zinn, J. (1994). Wherever You Go, There You Are.

Nhat Hanh, T. (1999). The Miracle of Mindfulness.

On Self-Compassion & Inner Voice

Neff, K. (2015). Self-Compassion: The Proven Power of Being Kind to Yourself.

Germer, C. K. (2009). The Mindful Path to Self-Compassion.

On Resilience & Gratitude

Brown, B. (2015). Rising Strong.

Emmons, R. A. (2007). Thanks! How Practicing Gratitude Can Make You Happier.

On Living Boldly

Frankl, V. E. (1946). Man's Search for Meaning.

Seligman, M. (2011). Flourish: A Visionary New Understanding of Happiness and Well-being.

Quiet the Spiral Journal Page

1. Spiral Check-In
What thought is looping in my mind?

_____

2. Pause & Name It
This is just a thought about:

_____

3. Reframe It
A kinder or clearer way to see this is:

_____

4. Gratitude Grounding
One thing I'm grateful for right now:

_____

5. Moving Forward
One small action I can take next:

_____

Notes & Thoughts:

Quiet the Spiral Journal Page

1. Spiral Check-In
What thought is looping in my mind?

_____

2. Pause & Name It
This is just a thought about:

_____

3. Reframe It
A kinder or clearer way to see this is:

_____

4. Gratitude Grounding
One thing I'm grateful for right now:

_____

5. Moving Forward
One small action I can take next:

_____

Notes & Thoughts:

Quiet the Spiral Journal Page

1. Spiral Check-In
What thought is looping in my mind?

_____

2. Pause & Name It
This is just a thought about:

_____

3. Reframe It
A kinder or clearer way to see this is:

_____

4. Gratitude Grounding
One thing I'm grateful for right now:

_____

5. Moving Forward
One small action I can take next:

_____

Notes & Thoughts:

Quiet the Spiral Journal Page

1. Spiral Check-In
What thought is looping in my mind?

_____

2. Pause & Name It
This is just a thought about:

_____

3. Reframe It
A kinder or clearer way to see this is:

_____

4. Gratitude Grounding
One thing I'm grateful for right now:

_____

5. Moving Forward
One small action I can take next:

_____

Notes & Thoughts:

Quiet the Spiral Journal Page

1. Spiral Check-In
What thought is looping in my mind?

_____

2. Pause & Name It
This is just a thought about:

_____

3. Reframe It
A kinder or clearer way to see this is:

_____

4. Gratitude Grounding
One thing I'm grateful for right now:

_____

5. Moving Forward
One small action I can take next:

_____

Notes & Thoughts:

Quiet the Spiral Journal Page

1. Spiral Check-In
What thought is looping in my mind?

_____

2. Pause & Name It
This is just a thought about:

_____

3. Reframe It
A kinder or clearer way to see this is:

_____

4. Gratitude Grounding
One thing I'm grateful for right now:

_____

5. Moving Forward
One small action I can take next:

_____

Notes & Thoughts:

Quiet the Spiral Journal Page

1. Spiral Check-In
What thought is looping in my mind?

_____

2. Pause & Name It
This is just a thought about:

_____

3. Reframe It
A kinder or clearer way to see this is:

_____

4. Gratitude Grounding
One thing I'm grateful for right now:

_____

5. Moving Forward
One small action I can take next:

_____

Notes & Thoughts:

Quiet the Spiral Journal Page

1. Spiral Check-In
What thought is looping in my mind?

_____

2. Pause & Name It
This is just a thought about:

_____

3. Reframe It
A kinder or clearer way to see this is:

_____

4. Gratitude Grounding
One thing I'm grateful for right now:

_____

5. Moving Forward
One small action I can take next:

_____

Notes & Thoughts:

Quiet the Spiral Journal Page

1. Spiral Check-In
What thought is looping in my mind?

_____

2. Pause & Name It
This is just a thought about:

_____

3. Reframe It
A kinder or clearer way to see this is:

_____

4. Gratitude Grounding
One thing I'm grateful for right now:

_____

5. Moving Forward
One small action I can take next:

_____

Notes & Thoughts:

Quiet the Spiral Journal Page

1. Spiral Check-In
What thought is looping in my mind?

_____

2. Pause & Name It
This is just a thought about:

_____

3. Reframe It
A kinder or clearer way to see this is:

_____

4. Gratitude Grounding
One thing I'm grateful for right now:

_____

5. Moving Forward
One small action I can take next:

_____

Notes & Thoughts:

Quiet the Spiral Journal Page

1. Spiral Check-In
What thought is looping in my mind?

_____

2. Pause & Name It
This is just a thought about:

_____

3. Reframe It
A kinder or clearer way to see this is:

_____

4. Gratitude Grounding
One thing I'm grateful for right now:

_____

5. Moving Forward
One small action I can take next:

_____

Notes & Thoughts:

Quiet the Spiral Journal Page

1. Spiral Check-In
What thought is looping in my mind?

_____

2. Pause & Name It
This is just a thought about:

_____

3. Reframe It
A kinder or clearer way to see this is:

_____

4. Gratitude Grounding
One thing I'm grateful for right now:

_____

5. Moving Forward
One small action I can take next:

_____

Notes & Thoughts:

Quiet the Spiral Journal Page

1. Spiral Check-In

What thought is looping in my mind?

_____

2. Pause & Name It

This is just a thought about:

_____

3. Reframe It

A kinder or clearer way to see this is:

_____

4. Gratitude Grounding

One thing I'm grateful for right now:

_____

5. Moving Forward

One small action I can take next:

_____

Notes & Thoughts:

Quiet the Spiral Journal Page

1. Spiral Check-In
What thought is looping in my mind?

_____

2. Pause & Name It
This is just a thought about:

_____

3. Reframe It
A kinder or clearer way to see this is:

_____

4. Gratitude Grounding
One thing I'm grateful for right now:

_____

5. Moving Forward
One small action I can take next:

_____

Notes & Thoughts:

Quiet the Spiral Journal Page

1. Spiral Check-In
What thought is looping in my mind?

_____

2. Pause & Name It
This is just a thought about:

_____

3. Reframe It
A kinder or clearer way to see this is:

_____

4. Gratitude Grounding
One thing I'm grateful for right now:

_____

5. Moving Forward
One small action I can take next:

_____

Notes & Thoughts:

Quiet the Spiral Journal Page

1. Spiral Check-In
What thought is looping in my mind?

_____

2. Pause & Name It
This is just a thought about:

_____

3. Reframe It
A kinder or clearer way to see this is:

_____

4. Gratitude Grounding
One thing I'm grateful for right now:

_____

5. Moving Forward
One small action I can take next:

_____

Notes & Thoughts:

Quiet the Spiral Journal Page

1. Spiral Check-In
What thought is looping in my mind?

_____

2. Pause & Name It
This is just a thought about:

_____

3. Reframe It
A kinder or clearer way to see this is:

_____

4. Gratitude Grounding
One thing I'm grateful for right now:

_____

5. Moving Forward
One small action I can take next:

_____

Notes & Thoughts:

Quiet the Spiral Journal Page

1. Spiral Check-In
What thought is looping in my mind?

_____

2. Pause & Name It
This is just a thought about:

_____

3. Reframe It
A kinder or clearer way to see this is:

_____

4. Gratitude Grounding
One thing I'm grateful for right now:

_____

5. Moving Forward
One small action I can take next:

_____

Notes & Thoughts:

Quiet the Spiral Journal Page

1. Spiral Check-In
What thought is looping in my mind?

_____

2. Pause & Name It
This is just a thought about:

_____

3. Reframe It
A kinder or clearer way to see this is:

_____

4. Gratitude Grounding
One thing I'm grateful for right now:

_____

5. Moving Forward
One small action I can take next:

_____

Notes & Thoughts:

Quiet the Spiral Journal Page

1. Spiral Check-In
What thought is looping in my mind?

_____

2. Pause & Name It
This is just a thought about:

_____

3. Reframe It
A kinder or clearer way to see this is:

_____

4. Gratitude Grounding
One thing I'm grateful for right now:

_____

5. Moving Forward
One small action I can take next:

_____

Notes & Thoughts:

Quiet the Spiral Journal Page

1. Spiral Check-In
What thought is looping in my mind?

_____

2. Pause & Name It
This is just a thought about:

_____

3. Reframe It
A kinder or clearer way to see this is:

_____

4. Gratitude Grounding
One thing I'm grateful for right now:

_____

5. Moving Forward
One small action I can take next:

_____

Notes & Thoughts:

Quiet the Spiral Journal Page

1. Spiral Check-In
What thought is looping in my mind?

_____

2. Pause & Name It
This is just a thought about:

_____

3. Reframe It
A kinder or clearer way to see this is:

_____

4. Gratitude Grounding
One thing I'm grateful for right now:

_____

5. Moving Forward
One small action I can take next:

_____

Notes & Thoughts:

Quiet the Spiral Journal Page

1. Spiral Check-In

What thought is looping in my mind?

_____

2. Pause & Name It

This is just a thought about:

_____

3. Reframe It

A kinder or clearer way to see this is:

_____

4. Gratitude Grounding

One thing I'm grateful for right now:

_____

5. Moving Forward

One small action I can take next:

_____

Notes & Thoughts:

Quiet the Spiral Journal Page

1. Spiral Check-In
What thought is looping in my mind?

_____

2. Pause & Name It
This is just a thought about:

_____

3. Reframe It
A kinder or clearer way to see this is:

_____

4. Gratitude Grounding
One thing I'm grateful for right now:

_____

5. Moving Forward
One small action I can take next:

_____

Notes & Thoughts:

Quiet the Spiral Journal Page

1. Spiral Check-In
What thought is looping in my mind?

_____

2. Pause & Name It
This is just a thought about:

_____

3. Reframe It
A kinder or clearer way to see this is:

_____

4. Gratitude Grounding
One thing I'm grateful for right now:

_____

5. Moving Forward
One small action I can take next:

_____

Notes & Thoughts:

Quiet the Spiral Journal Page

1. Spiral Check-In
What thought is looping in my mind?

_____

2. Pause & Name It
This is just a thought about:

_____

3. Reframe It
A kinder or clearer way to see this is:

_____

4. Gratitude Grounding
One thing I'm grateful for right now:

_____

5. Moving Forward
One small action I can take next:

_____

Notes & Thoughts:

Quiet the Spiral Journal Page

1. Spiral Check-In
What thought is looping in my mind?

_____

2. Pause & Name It
This is just a thought about:

_____

3. Reframe It
A kinder or clearer way to see this is:

_____

4. Gratitude Grounding
One thing I'm grateful for right now:

_____

5. Moving Forward
One small action I can take next:

_____

Notes & Thoughts:

Quiet the Spiral Journal Page

1. Spiral Check-In
What thought is looping in my mind?

_____

2. Pause & Name It
This is just a thought about:

_____

3. Reframe It
A kinder or clearer way to see this is:

_____

4. Gratitude Grounding
One thing I'm grateful for right now:

_____

5. Moving Forward
One small action I can take next:

_____

Notes & Thoughts:

Quiet the Spiral Journal Page

1. Spiral Check-In
What thought is looping in my mind?

_____

2. Pause & Name It
This is just a thought about:

_____

3. Reframe It
A kinder or clearer way to see this is:

_____

4. Gratitude Grounding
One thing I'm grateful for right now:

_____

5. Moving Forward
One small action I can take next:

_____

Notes & Thoughts:

Quiet the Spiral Journal Page

1. Spiral Check-In
What thought is looping in my mind?

_____

2. Pause & Name It
This is just a thought about:

_____

3. Reframe It
A kinder or clearer way to see this is:

_____

4. Gratitude Grounding
One thing I'm grateful for right now:

_____

5. Moving Forward
One small action I can take next:

_____

Notes & Thoughts:

Quiet the Spiral Journal Page

1. Spiral Check-In
What thought is looping in my mind?

_____

2. Pause & Name It
This is just a thought about:

_____

3. Reframe It
A kinder or clearer way to see this is:

_____

4. Gratitude Grounding
One thing I'm grateful for right now:

_____

5. Moving Forward
One small action I can take next:

_____

Notes & Thoughts:

Quiet the Spiral Journal Page

1. Spiral Check-In
What thought is looping in my mind?

_____

2. Pause & Name It
This is just a thought about:

_____

3. Reframe It
A kinder or clearer way to see this is:

_____

4. Gratitude Grounding
One thing I'm grateful for right now:

_____

5. Moving Forward
One small action I can take next:

_____

Notes & Thoughts:

Quiet the Spiral Journal Page

1. Spiral Check-In
What thought is looping in my mind?

_____

2. Pause & Name It
This is just a thought about:

_____

3. Reframe It
A kinder or clearer way to see this is:

_____

4. Gratitude Grounding
One thing I'm grateful for right now:

_____

5. Moving Forward
One small action I can take next:

_____

Notes & Thoughts:

Quiet the Spiral Journal Page

1. Spiral Check-In
What thought is looping in my mind?

_____

2. Pause & Name It
This is just a thought about:

_____

3. Reframe It
A kinder or clearer way to see this is:

_____

4. Gratitude Grounding
One thing I'm grateful for right now:

_____

5. Moving Forward
One small action I can take next:

_____

Notes & Thoughts:

Quiet the Spiral Journal Page

1. Spiral Check-In
What thought is looping in my mind?

_____

2. Pause & Name It
This is just a thought about:

_____

3. Reframe It
A kinder or clearer way to see this is:

_____

4. Gratitude Grounding
One thing I'm grateful for right now:

_____

5. Moving Forward
One small action I can take next:

_____

Notes & Thoughts:

Quiet the Spiral Journal Page

1. Spiral Check-In
What thought is looping in my mind?

_____

2. Pause & Name It
This is just a thought about:

_____

3. Reframe It
A kinder or clearer way to see this is:

_____

4. Gratitude Grounding
One thing I'm grateful for right now:

_____

5. Moving Forward
One small action I can take next:

_____

Notes & Thoughts:

Quiet the Spiral Journal Page

1. Spiral Check-In
What thought is looping in my mind?

_____

2. Pause & Name It
This is just a thought about:

_____

3. Reframe It
A kinder or clearer way to see this is:

_____

4. Gratitude Grounding
One thing I'm grateful for right now:

_____

5. Moving Forward
One small action I can take next:

_____

Notes & Thoughts:

Quiet the Spiral Journal Page

1. Spiral Check-In
What thought is looping in my mind?

_____

2. Pause & Name It
This is just a thought about:

_____

3. Reframe It
A kinder or clearer way to see this is:

_____

4. Gratitude Grounding
One thing I'm grateful for right now:

_____

5. Moving Forward
One small action I can take next:

_____

Notes & Thoughts:

Quiet the Spiral Journal Page

1. Spiral Check-In
What thought is looping in my mind?

_____

2. Pause & Name It
This is just a thought about:

_____

3. Reframe It
A kinder or clearer way to see this is:

_____

4. Gratitude Grounding
One thing I'm grateful for right now:

_____

5. Moving Forward
One small action I can take next:

_____

Notes & Thoughts:

Quiet the Spiral Journal Page

1. Spiral Check-In

What thought is looping in my mind?

_____

2. Pause & Name It

This is just a thought about:

_____

3. Reframe It

A kinder or clearer way to see this is:

_____

4. Gratitude Grounding

One thing I'm grateful for right now:

_____

5. Moving Forward

One small action I can take next:

_____

Notes & Thoughts:

Quiet the Spiral Journal Page

1. Spiral Check-In
What thought is looping in my mind?

_____

2. Pause & Name It
This is just a thought about:

_____

3. Reframe It
A kinder or clearer way to see this is:

_____

4. Gratitude Grounding
One thing I'm grateful for right now:

_____

5. Moving Forward
One small action I can take next:

_____

Notes & Thoughts:

Quiet the Spiral Journal Page

1. Spiral Check-In
What thought is looping in my mind?

_____

2. Pause & Name It
This is just a thought about:

_____

3. Reframe It
A kinder or clearer way to see this is:

_____

4. Gratitude Grounding
One thing I'm grateful for right now:

_____

5. Moving Forward
One small action I can take next:

_____

Notes & Thoughts:

Quiet the Spiral Journal Page

1. Spiral Check-In
What thought is looping in my mind?

_____

2. Pause & Name It
This is just a thought about:

_____

3. Reframe It
A kinder or clearer way to see this is:

_____

4. Gratitude Grounding
One thing I'm grateful for right now:

_____

5. Moving Forward
One small action I can take next:

_____

Notes & Thoughts:

Quiet the Spiral Journal Page

1. Spiral Check-In
What thought is looping in my mind?

_____

2. Pause & Name It
This is just a thought about:

_____

3. Reframe It
A kinder or clearer way to see this is:

_____

4. Gratitude Grounding
One thing I'm grateful for right now:

_____

5. Moving Forward
One small action I can take next:

_____

Notes & Thoughts:

Quiet the Spiral Journal Page

1. Spiral Check-In
What thought is looping in my mind?

_____

2. Pause & Name It
This is just a thought about:

_____

3. Reframe It
A kinder or clearer way to see this is:

_____

4. Gratitude Grounding
One thing I'm grateful for right now:

_____

5. Moving Forward
One small action I can take next:

_____

Notes & Thoughts:

Quiet the Spiral Journal Page

1. Spiral Check-In
What thought is looping in my mind?
_____

2. Pause & Name It
This is just a thought about:
_____

3. Reframe It
A kinder or clearer way to see this is:
_____

4. Gratitude Grounding
One thing I'm grateful for right now:
_____

5. Moving Forward
One small action I can take next:
_____

Notes & Thoughts:

Quiet the Spiral Journal Page

1. Spiral Check-In
What thought is looping in my mind?

_____

2. Pause & Name It
This is just a thought about:

_____

3. Reframe It
A kinder or clearer way to see this is:

_____

4. Gratitude Grounding
One thing I'm grateful for right now:

_____

5. Moving Forward
One small action I can take next:

_____

Notes & Thoughts:

Quiet the Spiral Journal Page

1. Spiral Check-In

What thought is looping in my mind?

_____

2. Pause & Name It

This is just a thought about:

_____

3. Reframe It

A kinder or clearer way to see this is:

_____

4. Gratitude Grounding

One thing I'm grateful for right now:

_____

5. Moving Forward

One small action I can take next:

_____

Notes & Thoughts:

Quiet the Spiral Journal Page

1. Spiral Check-In
What thought is looping in my mind?

_____

2. Pause & Name It
This is just a thought about:

_____

3. Reframe It
A kinder or clearer way to see this is:

_____

4. Gratitude Grounding
One thing I'm grateful for right now:

_____

5. Moving Forward
One small action I can take next:

_____

Notes & Thoughts:

Quiet the Spiral Journal Page

1. Spiral Check-In
What thought is looping in my mind?

_____

2. Pause & Name It
This is just a thought about:

_____

3. Reframe It
A kinder or clearer way to see this is:

_____

4. Gratitude Grounding
One thing I'm grateful for right now:

_____

5. Moving Forward
One small action I can take next:

_____

Notes & Thoughts:

Quiet the Spiral Journal Page

1. Spiral Check-In
What thought is looping in my mind?

_____

2. Pause & Name It
This is just a thought about:

_____

3. Reframe It
A kinder or clearer way to see this is:

_____

4. Gratitude Grounding
One thing I'm grateful for right now:

_____

5. Moving Forward
One small action I can take next:

_____

Notes & Thoughts:

Quiet the Spiral Journal Page

1. Spiral Check-In
What thought is looping in my mind?

_____

2. Pause & Name It
This is just a thought about:

_____

3. Reframe It
A kinder or clearer way to see this is:

_____

4. Gratitude Grounding
One thing I'm grateful for right now:

_____

5. Moving Forward
One small action I can take next:

_____

Notes & Thoughts:

Quiet the Spiral Journal Page

1. Spiral Check-In
What thought is looping in my mind?

_____

2. Pause & Name It
This is just a thought about:

_____

3. Reframe It
A kinder or clearer way to see this is:

_____

4. Gratitude Grounding
One thing I'm grateful for right now:

_____

5. Moving Forward
One small action I can take next:

_____

Notes & Thoughts:

Quiet the Spiral Journal Page

1. Spiral Check-In
What thought is looping in my mind?
_____

2. Pause & Name It
This is just a thought about:
_____

3. Reframe It
A kinder or clearer way to see this is:
_____

4. Gratitude Grounding
One thing I'm grateful for right now:
_____

5. Moving Forward
One small action I can take next:
_____

Notes & Thoughts:

Quiet the Spiral Journal Page

1. Spiral Check-In
What thought is looping in my mind?

_____

2. Pause & Name It
This is just a thought about:

_____

3. Reframe It
A kinder or clearer way to see this is:

_____

4. Gratitude Grounding
One thing I'm grateful for right now:

_____

5. Moving Forward
One small action I can take next:

_____

Notes & Thoughts:

Quiet the Spiral Journal Page

1. Spiral Check-In
What thought is looping in my mind?

_____

2. Pause & Name It
This is just a thought about:

_____

3. Reframe It
A kinder or clearer way to see this is:

_____

4. Gratitude Grounding
One thing I'm grateful for right now:

_____

5. Moving Forward
One small action I can take next:

_____

Notes & Thoughts:

Quiet the Spiral Journal Page

1. Spiral Check-In
What thought is looping in my mind?

---

2. Pause & Name It
This is just a thought about:

---

3. Reframe It
A kinder or clearer way to see this is:

---

4. Gratitude Grounding
One thing I'm grateful for right now:

---

5. Moving Forward
One small action I can take next:

Notes & Thoughts:

Quiet the Spiral Journal Page

1. Spiral Check-In
What thought is looping in my mind?

_____

2. Pause & Name It
This is just a thought about:

_____

3. Reframe It
A kinder or clearer way to see this is:

_____

4. Gratitude Grounding
One thing I'm grateful for right now:

_____

5. Moving Forward
One small action I can take next:

_____

Notes & Thoughts:

Quiet the Spiral Journal Page

1. Spiral Check-In
What thought is looping in my mind?

_____

2. Pause & Name It
This is just a thought about:

_____

3. Reframe It
A kinder or clearer way to see this is:

_____

4. Gratitude Grounding
One thing I'm grateful for right now:

_____

5. Moving Forward
One small action I can take next:

_____

Notes & Thoughts:

Quiet the Spiral Journal Page

1. Spiral Check-In
What thought is looping in my mind?

_____

2. Pause & Name It
This is just a thought about:

_____

3. Reframe It
A kinder or clearer way to see this is:

_____

4. Gratitude Grounding
One thing I'm grateful for right now:

_____

5. Moving Forward
One small action I can take next:

_____

Notes & Thoughts:

Quiet the Spiral Journal Page

1. Spiral Check-In
What thought is looping in my mind?

_____

2. Pause & Name It
This is just a thought about:

_____

3. Reframe It
A kinder or clearer way to see this is:

_____

4. Gratitude Grounding
One thing I'm grateful for right now:

_____

5. Moving Forward
One small action I can take next:

_____

Notes & Thoughts:

www.ingramcontent.com/pod-product-compliance
Lightning Source LLC
La Vergne TN
LVHW051557080426
835510LV00020B/3012